Retire $ Richer Younger

A practical alternative to working until you are 67

Barbara Smith Ed Koken

major st
PUBLISHING

First published in 2010 by Major Street Publishing
© Barbara Smith and Ed Koken 2010
The moral rights of the authors have been asserted

National Library of Australia Cataloguing-in-Publication data:
Author: Smith, Barbara
Title: Retire richer younger: a practical alternative to working until you are 67
ISBN: 9780980756418 (pbk.)
Notes: Includes index.
Subjects: Retirement income – Australia.
        Retirement – Australia – Planning.
        Retirement – Australia.
Other Authors/Contributors: Koken, Ed.
Dewey Number: 332.02401

Internal design by Production Works
Cover design by Pipeline Design
Printed in Australia by Griffin Press
Reprinted 2012

10 9 8 7 6 5 4 3 2

Disclaimer
The material in this publication is of the nature of general comment only, and does not represent professional advice. It is not intended to provide specific guidance for particular circumstances and it should not be relied on as the basis for any decision to take action or not take action on any matter which it covers. Readers should obtain professional advice where appropriate, before making any such decision. To maximum extent permitted by law, the authors and publisher disclaim all responsibility and liability to any person, arising directly or indirectly from any person taking or not taking action based upon the information in this publication.

Contents

Preface

There is no prescribed retirement age in Australia however many people regard the age at which you can first apply for the age pension as 'retirement age'. This varies from age 64 to 67, depending upon when you were born and whether you are male or female. Do you really want to keep working that long?

In writing this book, our objective is to help you to start planning for your retirement. By saving and investing smartly from today on, your wealth will increase over time and you can retire when you choose to and live the lifestyle of your dreams.

Ed and I (Barbara speaking) have spent most of our working lives helping people prepare themselves financially for retirement. Whether it's been through the many books we have written on the subject, through our talks and seminars, or face to face with our clients, it has been our passion. It has also been a focus of our life partnership to set ourselves up financially so that we can enjoy ourselves when we retire and retire when we choose. It has been an interesting and educational journey, sometimes exciting and occasionally challenging and even scary.

By picking up this book you have decided to take firmer control of your retirement planning. So join us now as you embark upon your journey to a comfortable and secure retirement.

In order to avoid confusion throughout the book we have used the word 'pension' where we are referring to a pension paid by the commonwealth government and the words 'income stream' where we are referring to superannuation or self-funded regular income payments.

We have included an Appendix at the end of the book which gives the thresholds and deeming rates at time of writing. If you are reading this book some time after the publication date you can find up-to-date superannuation rates on the Australian Taxation Office (ATO) website at www.ato.gov.au. Current social security thresholds and deeming rates are on the Centrelink website at www.centrelink.gov.au.

Barbara Smith and Ed Koken
www.oasiswealth.com.au
Melbourne, March 2010

Readers of this book are enititled to a free one-year subscription to the authors' quarterly eNewsSheet. Just send an email with the subject line "Free subscription for 1 year" to superbsmith@optusnet.com.au. Please note that emails sent to this address are not opened.

CHAPTER 1

It's your future so plan it now

In this chapter you will learn:
- What is involved in retirement planning
- How to get started.

I t's never too early or too late to start planning for retirement. The sooner you start building assets, the earlier you can retire, and the more likely you are to be able to fully self-fund your retirement. If you haven't already started you can't change the past but can begin now! Whether you are 21 or 61, this book is designed to assist you in planning for an earlier retirement date and a more financially secure retirement. So, let's get started and look at what planning for an early retirement may entail.

One definition of retirement is "the state of being retired from one's business or occupation". This could be due to a variety of reasons such as personal choice, health or economic circumstances. However the definition of retirement is evolving as people live longer and have more retirement choices. You may retire from a structured working life to pursue another career that offers greater flexibility and freedom in your schedule; or you may choose to follow personal interests or undertake community service. We consider retirement means doing what you *want* to do, not what you *need* to do. The modern definition of retirement has more to do with *re-engaging* than *disengaging*.

However, as your retirement plans take shape, they will need to be funded. Retirement planning involves accumulating investment assets which will generate a steady income to fund your desired lifestyle. It will give you financial independence allowing employment to be an option rather than a necessity.

There are two major errors many people make when they embark upon retirement planning. The first is they fail to set specific goals (financial and lifestyle). The second is that they defer investing to just before retirement. When you set out to achieve any goal in life, you are far more likely to succeed if you have a simple plan. This is especially important in relation to retirement planning because once you retire there is usually less time and there are fewer opportunities to increase your wealth. Your retirement savings will continue to increase in value if you invest wisely in an appropriate selection of assets and income streams, but the earlier you start and the better your plan, the easier the whole process will be.

If you intend to rely on the government to fund your retirement, you may have to wait until you reach age 67. In addition you will be forced to cope with ever changing rules that seem to be designed to exclude more people from qualifying for government income support.

Is that really what you want?

People are living longer, healthier lives. If you don't want to rely solely on the age pension for your income it is time to get planning your future finances now.

WHAT IS INVOLVED IN RETIREMENT PLANNING?

Throughout this book we will show you how to formulate your plan and make it work for you. The questions we answer the most in our work with clients and investors are:

— How much have I got already?
— How much will I need?
— How can I achieve my financial goals earlier?
— What do I need to do when I retire?

When you have the answers to these questions you have the makings of a sound plan in place and you will be well on the road to financial independence in retirement.

Planning for retirement, both from a lifestyle and financial perspective should be part of the ongoing wealth creation process. Some people get hooked on tax deductions and they can be valuable, but only if they also pay attention to the quality and mix of their investments both now and in the future.

How much have I got already?

People are often amazed at what they already have and their income generating and savings capacity. Too many people fritter away all of their income without setting anything aside as part of their early retirement plans. If their retirement income planning has been limited to their employer's superannuation contributions they need to stop and think more carefully about their future plans and how they can achieve them.

The first step to working out how much you have is to check your superannuation fund balance and look at the fund's performance. Most funds will send you a member's benefit statement twice yearly detailing contributions, investment returns, fees, any insurances and giving you your balance. If you are not receiving this you need to find out from your employer who is managing your fund, then contact the fund to make sure they have your most up-to-date contact details. This statement will also outline the investment mix your fund has adopted for you. If, after reviewing this information, you are concerned that your fund is not performing, or is going backwards, you may have made the wrong investment choices, or it may just be a poorly performing fund. In either case you will be in for a bleak future if this is all the retirement savings you have.

If you are already saving for your retirement and perhaps adding to your employer's contributions that's a great start. As well as your superannuation savings you will have other assets. In chapter 3 we show you how to draw up a net assets statement detailing what you own and what you owe.

How much will I need?

The next step is to work out how much you need in retirement to continue with your current lifestyle. You may be one of the many people who will spend as much time, if not more, in retirement than you have spent working. You might even make it to a hundred – a challenging thought! Even if you have a fair amount of money will it last for that period of time? Throughout the book we look at various ways of assessing how much is enough. We also show you early on how, by budgeting and putting a regular savings plan in place, you will reach your investment goals quicker.

One of the reasons for saving money is to invest in assets that will earn income and grow in value over time. Eventually these investments will provide you with an alternative or additional stream of income to that which you receive from working. If you plan properly this 'unearned' income will enable you to 'self-fund' your retirement at an earlier age than the government decrees. You will be able to do the things you have dreamed of during your working life sooner.

How can I achieve my goals sooner?

The way you invest and manage your superannuation savings plays an important part in how quickly you achieve your retirement planning goals. You need to work out the likely returns on your investments over time, both in terms of income and capital growth. It is important for your future wealth that you take time to look at, and understand, the possible outcomes of the investment mix you have selected in your current superannuation fund. If you are running your own self managed superannuation fund you need to take the time to understand how you can use it most effectively to build your retirement nest-egg.

Even if you are already saving for your retirement, work out how much you need to retire and maintain your current lifestyle. Then consider how you can achieve this savings goal by the date when you would like to retire. Whilst they are important at any age, these issues become more and more important as you get closer to your desired retirement age.

Compounding can have a powerful effect on savings and wealth creation. Einstein said that "the law of compound interest is the greatest tool available to mankind". We discuss compounding in chapter 2, but basically the earlier you start saving and investing for your retirement, the more you will benefit from compounding.

What do I need to do when I retire?

As you approach retirement, common wisdom accepts that you should only invest conservatively and preserve your capital against market crises. However, this is at the risk of losing the purchasing power of your capital during retirement. For example if you convert all of your real estate and share investments to fixed interest investments at retirement, in order to protect capital, you are guaranteeing that your standard of living will fall. Over time inflation will reduce the purchasing power of the income produced by fixed-interest bearing accounts. As a result you will either need to use up more and more capital earlier than necessary, or reduce your desired standard of living during your retirement years. Investing in a range of quality assets is one of the keys to protecting your longer-term capital and income. This is called diversification and we will discuss this in more detail later.

Whilst it is important to come to terms with the fact that you will inevitably have to use some of your capital to supplement your income once you are no longer working, it is still important to have some investments in assets that can continue to grow in value.

When you reach the age that you can access some or all of your superannuation (called your preservation age) you need to decide whether you should withdraw some or all of your superannuation benefits. Should you withdraw them as an income stream or as one or more lump sums? If you choose the lump sum option, you will then need to decide how you will invest or spend that money. All these options are covered later in this book.

Many people plan for the 'big trip of a lifetime' upon retirement. They spend a huge amount of money on this with little regard to how they will manage in their retirement years that follow. Planning your retirement is far more than planning a big trip. It is therefore important to have accumulated as much savings and as many assets, both inside and outside of superannuation, as are necessary to support your long-term plans after you retire. When you are confident that you have done this, then you may also consider opportunities to take that 'big trip' or several smaller trips.

BUSINESS MATTERS

So far our discussion has been general. Everyone's circumstances are different. Perhaps one of the biggest differences that can affect your retirement planning is whether you are an employee or self-employed, a professional or a small business operator. If you are in the latter group, your planning will have to take into account selling or closing your business. It is important to map out your plan as soon as possible, so that you maximise your hard-earned dollars for your retirement.

If you are a small business owner there are tax breaks available if you make a capital gain on the sale of your business assets. You need to discuss the latest rules with your accountant and/or financial adviser so that you can maximise the benefits available to your circumstances.

GETTING STARTED

Despite our enthusiasm for retirement planning from an early age we accept that many people put theirs off. Most people start thinking seriously about planning their income after retirement within 10 years of retirement. If you started earlier than this perhaps some major event in your life was a trigger. You may have lost your job or experienced a relationship breakdown. There may have been a death in the family which led to you receiving an inheritance. Where there is a triggering event there may be accompanying financial issues that can be quite complex and come with a range of alternatives and possibilities that you haven't even thought of.

To start your retirement planning write down as many ideas that would enhance your retirement if only you had enough money. Forget about things over which you have no control such as receiving a large inheritance from a distant relative.

Your retirement plans should include a variety of things both large and small. They may range from pursuing a neglected hobby to taking a short holiday within Australia or longer holidays overseas. Perhaps it's making time for renewing old friendships and making new friends. It may be about spending more time with your spouse, grandchildren or relatives, or doing some voluntary work. If you are a member of a couple then each of you should complete a separate wish list and then compare them. It is quite likely that you won't agree with each other on every item, if so, don't make it a problem, talk about it and find solutions.

Don't leave your planning any longer. Start now!

CHAPTER 2

Planning for your early retirement

In this chapter you will learn about:

- Your future income
- How much retirement income you will need
- How to maximise retirement income
- The power of regular savings
- Compounding returns
- How long your retirement savings will last.

The age pension in Australia is available as a safety net for older people who are unable to fully support themselves financially in retirement. It is paid to men when they reach age 65 to 67 and to women who are age 64 to 67. (You can check your age pension age in Table 8.1 in chapter 8). The age pension is subject to both income and assets tests with the one that gives the lower pension being applied. It should be a part of your retirement planning in as much as you should be aware of it. However, if you plan ahead early enough and there are no unforeseen circumstances taking you off track, you should be able to self fund your desired lifestyle at your chosen retirement age, without relying on the age pension.

The age pension is often accepted as the only source of income to a wage-earner whose main asset is labour sold to an employer. Too many people show no interest in how their superannuation guarantee contributions, paid for by their employer, are invested. At retirement a disappointing amount of superannuation is taken as a lump sum of money and spent on depreciating creature comforts and a holiday.

The same can happen to higher income earners who live an extravagant lifestyle and fail to realise that they also need to invest for their future financial needs. Once the regular wage stops, life becomes an ongoing financial battle on a low income that is only adequate for the most frugal.

Retirement from full time work may not mean that you leave the workforce altogether. You may choose to start a new business or undertake a course of study. You may choose to continue to work part time well into your retirement, sharing your skills with others. Retirement is simply a change of career that allows you more time and flexibility for leisure and sports activities which can often improve or maintain your level of health.

Planning for your retirement income to support your post retirement lifestyle requires patience, self-restraint and responsible and informed decision-making to ensure that your savings work as hard for you as you have worked to build them.

The very fact that you have picked up this book suggests that you are not content to wait until retirement age and survive on the age pension.

YOUR FUTURE INCOME

Most people retire before they can afford to. They do not even bother to calculate how much they will need to live on when they decide to stop working. When you are planning for your financial future you need to consider the following questions:

— How can I successfully manage my money and assets during my working life so that I spend less than my income and then save and invest wisely?

— What steps can I take to reduce my debts, especially those with non-tax deductible interest such as my mortgage and credit cards?

— How much extra money should I contribute to superannuation in order to produce additional income for my early retirement?

— How much money do I need to save and invest to provide myself with enough regular income to fund a comfortable retirement?

— How can I invest my savings to get the best overall return in terms of both income and capital growth?

— Where can I get good financial information to assist me?

Not surprisingly many people find it difficult to budget and save their money while they are raising their children. Only as children grow up and leave the home (if they ever do!) do they start to think about their retirement. In some cases this may be too late to achieve sufficient retirement income to retire as early as they would like to. However, it may still be possible to retire or semi-retire earlier than age pension age. And it may also be possible to claim a part age pension to compensate for inadequate self funded income.

Sources of income in retirement

Most people expect their main source of retirement income to come from superannuation, the age or service pension, and/or income from business, property or investment. Some people have no idea where their retirement income will come from!

The main ways of getting money that will give us that income in retirement are shown in the following diagram:

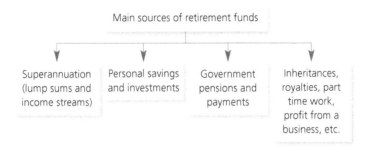

The order has no significance. Some of you may get money from all four sources, others from one or two. As part of your retirement planning you should consider all the different sources of income that could help to fund your retirement income needs. Different sources of income include:

— Interest from banks and other financial institutions

— Dividends from shares

— Rental income from investment properties

— Income from managed investments which are generally distributions of trust income, foreign income and capital gains

— Interest coupon payments from bonds

— Income streams from private sources including superannuation and non-superannuation sources (sometimes called self funded pensions or annuities)

— Part-time work

— Profits from a business

— Royalty income from books, copyrights, films, etc.

— Commonwealth government funded income such as the age pension, service pension, seniors supplement, etc.

— Inheritances

— Gifts from family members including children (rare but miracles sometimes happen!)

— Other income.

Getting income from more than one source and type of investment is called diversification of income and is a very important part of wealth creation and preservation. The secret of financial wealth is to have multiple income streams, each one of them enough for you to live on.

Costs in retirement

Your standard of living in retirement depends as much on your living costs as your income. Each person is different and has different spending habits. The essential rule to follow is to always ensure that you spend less than your income, otherwise it is very easy for your debt level to spiral out of control. Living costs include food, transport, leisure and entertainment, health and medical expenses, household goods and services, clothing, footwear, gifts, communications and property outgoings, such as council and water rates and gas and electricity. Before you retire you need to assess these costs and review them regularly, recognising that the mix of costs may change as you age and that your income may also change over time.

HOW MUCH RETIREMENT INCOME DO YOU NEED?

Your level of savings to fund your retirement income depends on your income, expenses and superannuation contributions throughout your working life. As a rule of thumb, you need 70 to 80 per cent of your employment income before retirement during retirement. If you start planning early it is possible to achieve the same amount or even greater income during retirement than your after-tax income while you were employed. However 70 to 80 per cent generally allows you to maintain a comfortable lifestyle.

The amount of retirement savings required to provide you with an ongoing retirement income stream can be calculated using the following formula:

Retirement savings required = 15 to 20 x net annual retirement income

This formula provides you with a ball park figure of how much money you should save for retirement.

CASE STUDY: Retirement savings required

Bob and Shirley are 62 years old and they are planning to retire within three months. They would like to have an income of $50,000 per annum net of tax to maintain their lifestyle during retirement. They have an outstanding mortgage of $50,000 on their rental property which they would like to pay off when they retire. They plan to live in their current home as long as their health remains good and then if necessary will move into a retirement village with a nursing home.

They have the following assets with current market values:

Residential home	$400,000
Superannuation (Bob)	$350,000
Superannuation (Shirley)	$150,000
Beach house (joint)	$220,000
Shares (joint)	$200,000
Bank account (joint)	$3,000
Rental property (CBD unit)	$150,000
Total	**$1,473,000**

A residential home is generally treated as a lifestyle asset and if we take away their home and the $50,000 mortgage from their total assets, they have $1,023,000.

Let's revisit our formula. Retirement savings required:

= 15 to 20 x net annual retirement income
= 15 to 20 x $50,000 = $750,000 to $1,000,000

As a ball park figure they appear to have sufficient assets to provide for the retirement income they desire. In this example we have ignored the income they can produce from their investments, possible taxes and charges on their non-superannuation income and other property assets, and the time value of money.

HOW TO MAXIMISE RETIREMENT INCOME

There are several ways you can improve your chances of having a good level of income in retirement. You may not be able to take all of these actions, however even some of them will help you to increase your chances over the long term of maximising your retirement income. These strategies include:

— Maximising your savings by starting to save early in your working life.

— Working as many years as you can and investing wisely in order to maximise your savings. Your retirement savings are affected by how much and how long you save and the after-tax return on your investments. Early retirement and redundancy while you are in the workforce will reduce your retirement savings capacity unless you are able to earn income from other sources.

— Obtaining the highest level of initial education possible and continuing this education through employment or business-based training. This will help you to obtain well-paid employment at all stages of your life. One word of caution: too much education may result in loss of time and a large student loan that will be repayable through the tax system if you spend many years in higher education.

— Actively managing your money and investments to maximise the return from them using the power of compounding. You may choose to invest directly into a variety of investments including shares, property and managed funds. This will diversify your risk as the market goes through changing cycles.

— Choosing investments that you are most comfortable with and closely following their performance. Always do your homework before investing your hard-earned money. Most people lose their money if they invest after only limited research. If you do make a bad investment or get duped – most of us do at some time or another – don't let the loss discourage or overwhelm you, continue with your retirement plan.

— Diversifying – never putting too much money into one type of investment will limit losses if that type goes bad.

Power of regular saving

Unfortunately, some people don't start thinking about a financial plan for retirement until they're just about ready to retire. That adds a lot of unnecessary stress to their lives. You can avoid having retirement sneak up on you by making a structured plan early. Remember, the sooner you start preparing for retirement and the more thoroughly you plan, the more likely you are to have sufficient money to enjoy yourself when retirement actually comes.

The following table shows the future growth potential of saving $100 per month in a savings plan, share portfolio or managed fund over a number of years and with different rates of return (income, capital growth or a combination of both).

Table 2.1 Accumulation of $100 invested per month at different rates of return and different time periods

Rate of return*	Number of years					
	5	10	15	20	25	30
5%	$6,801	$15,528	$26,729	$41,103	$59,551	$83,226
6%	$6,977	$16,388	$29,082	$46,204	$69,299	$100,452
7%	$7,159	$17,308	$31,696	$52,093	$81,007	$121,997
8%	$7,348	$18,295	$34,604	$58,902	$95,103	$149,036
9%	$7,542	$19,351	$37,841	$66,789	$112,112	$183,074
10%	$7,744	$20,484	$41,447	$75,937	$132,683	$226,049

*Note that this chart does not reflect the effect of taxes.

You can see from Table 2.1 that saving and investing $100 per month at a 6 per cent return provides a saving amount of $29,082 over a 15 year period. Of course, the higher the return on investment, the higher the final amount would be. This table is used for illustrative purposes only, as the rate of return from most investments varies over time.

Compounding returns

The 'miracle' of compounding is a powerful tool for investors. The driving force behind every successful investment is compounding earnings such as interest, where you earn interest on reinvested interest. Compound interest can work by starting your investment early and reinvesting your investment returns, rather than receiving them as cash and spending them. Investment returns can include dividends from shares, interest from fixed-interest accounts and rent from investment properties. You can automatically reinvest dividends by electing to join a dividend reinvestment plan. Interest can be automatically credited to your interest bearing accounts.

Let's take a look at some examples of the miracle of compounding.

Example 1: You invest $10,000 net of tax into your superannuation fund account. Assume the fund tax rate is 15 per cent, the inflation rate is 3 per cent and the earnings rate is 6.5 per cent. The following table shows the projections of investment outcomes for a range of periods.

Table 2.2 **$10,000 invested in superannuation over 1 to 30 years**

Year	Future value of superannuation savings including original $10,000
1	$10,536
5	$12,983
10	$16,855
15	$21,882
20	$28,409
25	$36,882
30	$47,883

Example 2: You invest $1,000 at 10 per cent per annum. At the end of the first year you receive interest of $100. If you reinvest this interest, at the end of the second year, you earn interest on $1,100, being $110. So your total value would now be $1,210. Each year you're earning interest on your original capital and your accumulated returns. The longer you hold your investment, the greater the impact of compound returns.

Example 3: Assume that you invest $10,000 now at 5 per cent annual return until age 65, the value of your investment varies depending on when you start investing. How much will you get back?

Age when you started the $10,000 investment	Value of investment (before tax)
Age 20	$89,850
Age 30	$55,160
Age 40	$33,865
Age 50	$20,790

As you can notice, you need to start an early saving and investing program so that your retirement wealth grows.

CASE STUDY: Comparison of two investments

Helen and Carolyn are twin sisters, and since they come from a financially prudent family both started a saving and investment plan, but at different ages. Helen started investing at the age of 20 and Carolyn at the age of 30. Carolyn spent her money travelling overseas before she settled down to have a family.

The sisters each contributed $3,000 a year and both reinvested their investment earnings. Their investments earned 5 per cent per annum.

Helen decided to stop contributing at the age of 50 but left her investment in place. Carolyn continued her regular investment plan right up till age 60. Who has the most money at age 60?

	Helen	Carolyn
Amount invested	$90,000	$90,000
Years invested	30	30
Annual return	5%	5%
Account value at age 60	$324,665	$199,316

Helen's money has grown to $324,665 while Carolyn, who invested the same amount but started saving 10 years later, ends up with considerably less, $199,316. This example does not include tax and also the rate of return is assumed constant. As we all know, rates of return on investments change over time.

The reason why Helen has a greater account balance, while investing the same amount as her sister over the same number of years, is that she started earlier to invest. Compounding had a greater effect on her earnings.

HOW LONG WILL YOUR RETIREMENT SAVINGS LAST?

This is an important question that most people are concerned about when they are planning for their retirement. In most cases, the size of the retirement nest-egg that will guarantee the desired retirement lifestyle is not carefully determined early enough. For some people it is too late since their lifestyle during their working lives has involved spending all of their income (and sometimes more) and saving little or nothing. This causes disappointment for some and they either continue to work longer to save for retirement or reduce their lifestyle dramatically in retirement. The government age pension alone is not sufficient to support any more than a basic retirement lifestyle.

The reality is that it is impossible for us to give you an exact answer to the question "how long will my retirement savings last?" because it depends on a whole range of factors. For example, you may choose to grow your own vegetables and make your own wine, and holiday with relatives to keep expenses low. Alternatively you may choose to eat out in expensive restaurants and travel and stay in expensive hotels.

There will also be factors outside of your control, including:

— How long you live after retirement. This may be only a short time or up to 40 years!

— Your health and the costs involved in dealing with your health needs.

— Inflation rates over many years. (Remember inflation is a silent killer of your money's buying power. For example, the cost of a loaf of bread is $3 today and it will be at least $4.50 in 10 years time, even with a low inflation rate of 4 per cent.)

— The income you can earn on your investments. You can control this to some extent if you purchase an income stream that guarantees income for your lifetime. But then the income is usually fairly low compared with the capital used to buy it.

— Whether your investments grow or fall in real value, or even disappear. This is of particular importance for pre-retirees who are accumulating wealth for retirement. It is also equally important for retirees who invest their savings as a retirement income stream, such as in a superannuation funded account-based income stream.

Having just said that we can't predict how long each individual's retirement savings will last, we can give some indications. Table 2.3 summarises how long retirement savings will last based on earnings and the rate of retirement income withdrawal. At a given earnings rate, as the retirement income amount increases, the duration of retirement savings to diminish decreases.

Table 2.3 How long retirement savings will last

Account earnings rate (% pa)	Rate of capital withdrawal (% pa)*										
	6	7	8	9	10	11	12	13	14	15	16
	How many years your capital will last										
5	33	24	19	15	13	11	10	9	8	8	7
6		30	22	17	14	12	11	10	9	8	7
7			27	20	16	14	12	10	9	8	8
8				25	19	15	13	11	10	9	8
9					23	18	15	12	11	10	9
10						22	17	14	12	10	9
11							21	16	13	11	10
12								19	15	13	11

*Source: Adapted from BT Funds Management Limited. Assumes an initial application fee of 3 per cent and no income tax effect.

For example, from the table if you choose to withdraw your benefits as an account-based income stream, the minimum amount of withdrawals annually are calculated at a percentage based on your age on 1 July and the capital balance. If the capital in your income stream is earning 8 per cent per annum it will last for 25 years if you withdraw 9 per cent of the capital value each year. It will last 10 years if you withdraw 14 per cent of the capital value each year.

You can make your retirement savings last longer by ensuring that they are invested into carefully selected and monitored assets to provide income and capital return to grow their value.

INFLATION

Inflation is a measure of how your money loses its value over time. The following graph shows how the value of $10,000 in 1980 went down until year 2008. As you can see, inflation erodes the value of your money therefore you need to invest it to protect its purchasing power over time.

Fig. 2.1 How inflation reduces purchasing power of money ($10,000 in 1980 to 2008)

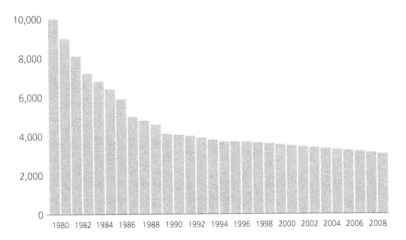

GROWTH INVESTMENT CHOICES FOR RETIREES

As we mentioned previously most retirees underestimate how much they will need in retirement. Also, wealth accumulation should not stop at retirement. Aggressive asset growth strategies are used by some pre retirees in an attempt to ensure that retirement savings last longer to provide retirement income for life. However, as you have witnessed in the recent global financial crisis this approach is fraught with danger, and large amounts of wealth have evaporated.

Aggressive growth strategies should be treated cautiously especially if you are conservative in nature and want to retain your capital, even if this means accepting a lower return. One option to consider is to invest part of your retirement savings into conservative assets such as term deposits to protect your capital. Then you can consider investing some of your money in growth assets that generate regular income such as shares with a good dividend yield and income producing property. Remember, however, when you invest your money into term deposits, your capital is protected but the buying power of your money is not. This is due to inflation which silently eats away at the value of your money.

When you do retire from work don't retire from investing. In fact once you do retire you should have more time to spend keeping track of investments and investment opportunities.

Carefully selected shares and property with the potential for capital growth can enable your retirement savings to increase in value. This will help you to preserve your assets and, if you desire, to pass them on to children and other dependants upon your death.

Growth assets have three major advantages when compared with term deposits:

— Carefully selected shares, property securities and investment properties can be tax effective and your capital has the potential to grow in value

— As your asset price rises in value, the dividends or rental income can increase to provide an inflation protected income stream

— For shares with franked dividends the tax credit can be used to reduce tax on other income.

Let's have a look at some case studies to illustrate our discussion on selecting at least some growth assets prior to and during retirement.

CASE STUDY 1: Term deposit versus share investments

Mary and Michael got married 20 years ago. Just before their wedding each had $10,000 in savings. Mary purchased 10,000 blue chip shares which paid a 4.2 per cent fully franked dividend each year. At the same time Michael, being a conservative person, decided it was important to protect his capital and so invested in a term deposit that paid 5 per cent per annum interest.

After 20 years their after-tax savings would be about $28,100 (original $10,000 plus dividends) for Mary and $16,900 for Michael and Mary's shares will probably have increased in value, meaning Mary is the more astute investor.

This is a simplified example since it assumes that dividend returns were constant and there was no increase or decrease in the value of the shares. There is always the possibility of shares decreasing in value and the risk of losing money on your investment when the share price falls. If you invest in shares you need to monitor their performance carefully.

CASE STUDY 2: A retirement plan to pay off debt and accumulate the required amount to retire early

Pauline is 49 years old and recently divorced. She does not have any children and she earns $70,000 a year. She has a debt of $100,000 on her rental property and she would like to pay it off well before her retirement. She has an investment portfolio which consists of:

Rental property	$300,000 (providing $300 per week gross rent)
Share portfolio	$110,000
Superannuation	$150,000
Total	$560,000

In order to keep things simple, we will use retirement money in today's dollars. She plans to retire at age 62 with $60,000 per year after-tax income to live on. She also wants to spend about $60,000 to renovate her home and purchase a new car at the time of her retirement.

Applying the 20 times net annual retirement income formula, Pauline needs about $1,200,000 to fund her retirement, renovate her house and purchase a new car at the time of retirement.

Using conservative estimates her net wealth at retirement will be as follows:

Asset	Value at retirement age of 62 (in today's dollars)
Investment property	$500,000
Share portfolio	$207,500
Superannuation (including contributions)	$370,000
Total	$1,077,500
Amount required for retirement	$1,200,000
Shortfall	$122,500

Pauline's taxable income is about $67,500 and she has a surplus of about $10,000 after-tax income annually. She can achieve her retirement goal by making additional superannuation contributions through salary sacrificing about $7,500 per annum (at an after-tax cost of about $5,000 per annum). The mortgage on her rental property can be paid well before her retirement with good budgeting, by paying her net rental income and her surplus after-tax income of about $5,000 each year into the mortgage. We have used conservative figures in this example and have assumed that she will continue to live in her residential home in her retirement. In some cases, people move into smaller homes or into a retirement village in their retirement years.

CHAPTER 3

Starting out on your retirement planning journey

In this chapter you will learn about:

- Assessing your net wealth
- Increasing your net wealth
- Analysing your personal statement of net wealth
- Analysing your current financial situation.

The overall goal of retirement planning is to understand your current financial situation and then find ways to build up the financial resources that you need to achieve your desired retirement lifestyle. Taking the next step on the road to an early retirement, in this chapter we start to assess your current financial situation. If, after this assessment, you find that your savings and investments are insufficient to provide your desired retirement lifestyle at your preferred date, we can help you develop a good retirement plan to still achieve your goals.

Your current financial position is the starting point. Figure 3.1, the early retirement road map (overleaf), is designed to lead you from where you are now to your chosen early retirement date.

Fig. 3.1 Early retirement road map

STEP 1 ▷ Evaluate your current personal and financial situation (establish where you are now and what your financial worth is)

STEP 2 ▷ Determine the financial and lifestyle goals that will result in an early retirement (decide where you want to be and when)

STEP 3 ▷ Develop and implement your early retirement plan (work out strategies and investment options that will get you there)

Your own early retirement plan is a journey from where you are today financially to where you would like to be financially at retirement and beyond. It is like having a road map and compass for your financial affairs. It gets you to evaluate where you are now and where you want to go in the future to achieve your retirement lifestyle goals. It then works out the options and strategies that you need to develop and implement in order to get you there. Be aware that if you detour from the route you map out in your plan you may still be able to get to where you intended financially, but your journey may be a little longer. You may encounter some unforeseen obstacles beyond your control that prevent you from reaching your planned financial destination. For example, you may suffer illness, retrenchment or a breakdown in a relationship. When this happens you will need to rethink your plan to deal with your changed circumstances.

So let's start planning your journey.

ASSESSING YOUR NET WEALTH

The starting point of the plan is to evaluate your current financial resources by preparing a statement of your net wealth. The sum of your total assets less your total liabilities is your net wealth, or in more simple language what you own minus what you owe is how much you are worth today.

Your assets (what you own) – Your liabilities (what you owe)
= Your current net worth (your net worth)

If you have ever applied for a mortgage or loan from a bank or other financial institution you might have filled out forms detailing what you owned and money that you owe to others. The bank is assessing your net wealth (and also your income and earnings capacity) so that it can assess whether to lend you money and if so, how much.

After you work out your current net wealth, the next step is to determine the amount of capital you need to produce the level of retirement income and lump sum expenditure you desire. The difference between your retirement net wealth and current net wealth is the shortfall or excess of capital (the amount of wealth you need to build, or the excess wealth you already have).

Required net wealth at retirement – Your current net wealth
= Shortfall or surplus of current net wealth

Statement of net wealth

A statement of net wealth is your personal balance sheet that records your assets and liabilities. It can help you assess your financial wealth and so help you to reach your retirement financial goals sooner. Most importantly it gives you information on how effectively your money is being used to create and accumulate wealth. It helps you to look carefully at how your money is currently invested. It provides you with a snapshot to review your overall assets, including investment assets, personal lifestyle assets, your liquid assets and your liabilities.

Your investment assets should be medium and long term investments that you are building up for the future. These may include term deposits, shares and real estate investments plus your retirement savings in superannuation.

Personal assets are those that you own for you and your family's enjoyment and lifestyle. They may include your family home, a holiday home, furniture and antiques, cars, boats and so on.

Liquid assets are the ones that can be converted to cash quickly, such as funds in your savings accounts, short-term investments and money market accounts.

Your statement of net wealth therefore also provides you with a quick method of checking whether your investments are sufficiently diversified into different asset classes.

On the liabilities side you can look at the types of debt and loans you have. Liabilities fall into two groups:

— Current liabilities which are to be paid in the near future. Examples include regular property outgoings, medical bills, insurance premiums, credit card debt and your tax bill.

— Long term liabilities which will not be paid within the coming year. A home or investment mortgage is a classic example of a long term liability.

You can put your statement of net wealth to use by highlighting any possible adjustments you need to make to improve your financial affairs and then proceed with an action plan.

Investment and lifestyle debt

Debts and loans from other people or financial institutions absorb income and become a burden to service when your income falls, particularly if it falls unexpectedly due to ill health or redundancy. Some people who fail to plan find themselves still owing large amounts of money when they would really like to retire from work. If you are approaching the time when you think you would like to retire and you have debts or loans it is very important to pay them off as quickly as possible so that by the time you do retire you are free from debt.

It is really important to set out your road map to retirement, and put in place a few financial strategies to help along the way. The following diagram can be used to help you to do just that.

Fig. 3.2 Financial strategies on the road to retirement

Repay debts – home loan, credit
cards, investment loans, etc.

Build super assets and non-super assets – cash, shares, property	Work out regular living expenses and capital expenses: new car, white goods, holidays	Work out income level and source – super income streams, income from investments, any government pension

Deductible and non-deductible debt

Your first priority in life is to get out of debt. This can be done by living about 15 per cent below your means; that means saving 15 per cent of your income to pay off your debts and later to invest. Debts can be divided into deductible and non-deductible debts for tax purposes.

Your retirement plan and wealth creation program should identify non-deductible debts that should be paid off first, since they do not give you any tax deductions. Start by paying off those with the highest interest rate so that your money works harder to create your wealth, not the wealth of the bank's shareholders.

For example, if you have a credit card debt of $5,000, with an annual interest rate is 15 per cent and you are making monthly repayments from your after-tax money, the real cost of that credit can be up to 29.1 per cent, depending on your marginal tax rate.

INCREASING YOUR NET WEALTH

One of your goals before you retire should be to increase your net wealth each year by a certain amount. Say one of your goals is to increase your net wealth by at least 10 per cent each year. How will you achieve this? Will you just hope for the best? Or will you use this financial plan to work out ways that it can be done, by setting strategies such as flexible budgeting, and saving and investing wisely for both income and growth.

As you go through your working life, ideally you start saving and investing in order to be able to live the lifestyle you desire after you retire. Figure 3.3 is a simplified graph that shows how the wealth you accumulate while you are in the workforce can generate retirement income after you retire. It illustrates how your retirement savings build up until you retire and then decline as you use both income and capital during your retirement years.

Fig. 3.3 Retirement savings curve

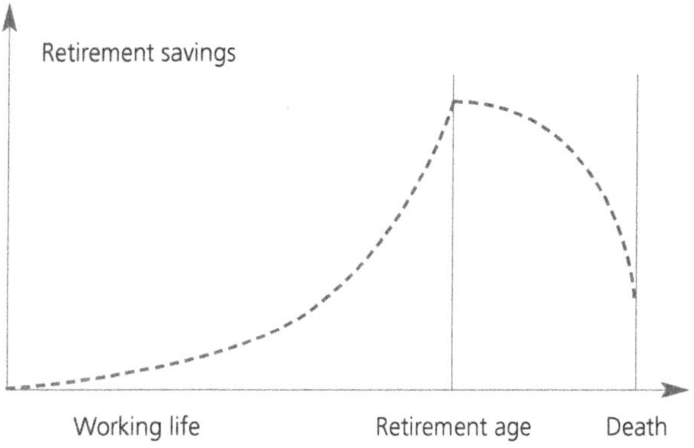

Some factors that affect how quickly and easily you can increase your net wealth are as follows:

— Personal budgeting and investment planning

— The age you start a savings plan

— The after-tax return on investments, changes in the economic and investment markets

— The age you finish education and start working

— Breaks in employment such as changing jobs, retrenchment, long term illness, injuries

— How long you continue to work before and during retirement

— Effective tax planning

— Whether you receive any windfalls or inheritances

— Changes in family circumstances such as, marriage, divorce, number of children

— The retirement age you select

— The type of retirement income stream you choose

— Whether you live longer than your estimated life expectancy.

Analysing your statement of net wealth

We have provided the following two forms for you to fill in as you assess your net wealth. You may photocopy these pages from the book.

The first form (3.1) should be used to detail your net wealth. Once you have completed your statement of net wealth you can gain a further insight from the information it contains by analysing it. Look at the net amount of assets or any deficiencies you have in each category of assets and complete Form 3.2.

It is important to be aware that even though you may have the same net wealth as another person the assets you own and the amount you owe may be totally different in value, growth potential and riskiness. Therefore your net wealth will almost certainly not be the same as the other person at a later date.

Form 3.1 Statement of Net Wealth

Date: _____ /_____ /20____

Your Assets (What You Own)

Assets	Current value ($)	% of total assets
PERSONAL LIFESTYLE ASSETS		
Family home		
Contents		
Motor vehicles		
Caravan, boat, other leisure assets		
Jewellery		
Holiday home		
Art, antiques and collectables		
Other personal assets		
Cash on hand		
Total personal assets		
LIQUID ASSETS		
Savings and cheque accounts		
Term deposits		
Cash management accounts		
Bank bills		
Credit Union and Building Society accounts		
Other		
Total liquid assets		
INVESTMENT ASSETS		
Shares		
Warrants/options		
Bonds		
Managed funds/Unit trusts		
Real estate		
Insurance/Friendly Society bonds		
Other		
Total investment assets		

SUPERANNUATION

Accumulated benefits

Rollovers

Superannuation income streams

Other superannuation benefits

Total superannuation assets

TOTAL ASSETS

Your Liabilities (What you Owe)

	Current	Deductible	%
LOANS, DEBTS AND COMMITTED EXPENDITURE			
Personal debt			
Car loan			
Home mortgage			
Boat loan			
Overdraft			
Loans you owe to other people			
Other personal debt			
Total personal debt			
SHORT-TERM LIABILITIES AND COMMITTED EXPENDITURE			
Credit card debts			
Income tax debts			
Planned travel			
Outstanding calls on warrants and options			
Other liabilities (list)			
Total short-term debt			
Investment debt			
Investment loan			
Margin loan			
Overdraft			
Other (list)			
Total investment debt			
TOTAL LIABILITIES			
NET WEALTH = Total Assets less			
Total Liabilities			

Form 3.2 Analysis of Net Wealth

Date: _____ /_____ /20____

Assets	$	%	Comments
PERSONAL ASSETS			
Total personal assets	_____	____	_____
Less personal debt	_____	____	_____
Equity in personal assets	_____	____	_____
SHORT-TERM ASSETS			
Total short-term assets	_____	____	_____
Less short-term debt and committed expenditure	_____	____	_____
Excess (deficit) in liquid assets	_____	____	_____
INVESTMENT ASSETS			
Total investment assets	_____	____	_____
Less debt on investment assets	_____	____	_____
Equity in investment assets	_____	____	_____
Superannuation assets	_____	____	_____
NET WEALTH	_____	____	_____

CHAPTER 4

Budgeting for financial independence

In this chapter you will learn about:
- Understanding your spending habits
- Positive cash flow
- Keeping your budgeting on track
- Making your budget work
- Keys to budgeting success
- Tips for successful budgeting.

There is an old saying that money can't buy you happiness, and whilst there may be some truth in it, try getting old without it!

UNDERSTANDING YOUR SPENDING HABITS

Before you can start any savings or investment program you need to understand your spending habits. A realistic family budget can help you control your family's spending whilst you are working towards your early retirement goals. In order to achieve this, your living expenses must be less than your income so that you have what is referred to as 'positive cash flow'.

One of the most important things you need to do towards your early retirement planning is to take the time to draw up a monthly and annual budget. This will help you to develop a budgeting and saving discipline while you are in the workforce, so that you will be financially independent earlier in your life.

Most people do not have or maintain even a simple budget and therefore they do not understand why they have not built enough assets for a comfortable retirement. Remember many family problems and arguments originate from financial issues. If both partners have a similar approach to money management, then they can work together to save money while raising children.

A budget can help you achieve your financial goals because it shows you succinctly how much you currently earn from all sources, where you are spending your money and how much you can save based on your current income and expenditure. It therefore highlights any weaknesses so that you are able to take steps to correct them. Always keep in mind that your income must be more than your overall expenditure if you are to successfully build savings for your retirement.

POSITIVE CASH FLOW

Drawing up an accurate budget, and then sticking to it, will help you to focus on how much you earn and from where. Your income may include your salary or wage, or income from your business, interest, dividends, trust distributions and so on.

If you find sticking to your budget is sometimes difficult, then reward yourself once in a while with an inexpensive special treat. A special treat could be a short holiday, going out for dinner or buying yourself something special that appeals to you. If you can increase your savings temporarily to pay for this treat all the better.

It is important to live within your means. The two key factors to creating wealth for your early retirement are positive cash flow (i.e. incomings are greater than outgoings) and investing your savings wisely.

When your actual monthly income less your expenditure results in excess income, the difference between your earnings and spending shows you how much you can save in that month.

If your budget shows you are spending more than you earn you need to take immediate action to cut down your spending and/or increase your earnings. Special attention must be paid to credit card bills and mortgage repayments. Pay them before they are overdue in order to avoid penalty interest charges.

Generally your income will increase as your career progresses or your business expands. Develop the financial discipline not to increase your spending as you earn more. Instead view the additional income as an opportunity to reduce debt. For example, you may increase payments on your mortgage, which in itself is building your wealth by increasing the equity you have in your home. Alternatively you may decide to increase savings or invest the extra income. We see some people who earned millions of dollars during their working lives, but they are still broke. This is because they spent everything they earned and more!

Make sure your budget is realistic. The main purpose of a budget is to help you to:

— Live within your income level

— Spend money wisely by controlling your discretionary expenses and bargain hunting when you do need to spend to get more for your money

— Develop better money management habits for you and your family

— Save at least 10 to 20 per cent of your earnings to invest so that you can achieve the early retirement date you desire

— Be prepared and able to ride out any financial emergencies that may arise.

To recap, have a simple budget and stick to it. Most people live their entire lives without ever drawing up a budget and are unaware of how much they have earned and spent over their working life. They usually end up with far less savings for retirement than the people who have had a simple budget.

CASE STUDY: Diane and Chris's story

Diane and Chris are in their early 50s with three children who are 15, 20 and 26 years old. Two of their children are still financially dependent and living with them (and this may continue for several years yet!). Chris was the sole earner whilst the children were growing up, working as a self employed carpenter. Diane started to work part-time in a dress shop two years ago.

Money management is a constant problem in their home. They do not have enough money to last for the whole month, and they have been living on credit for years. This did not change even after Diane resumed work, because she has been spending extra money on travel, clothes (after all she does get a staff discount) and make-up. Chris is frustrated about needing to budget to meet their living expenses.

The couple realise that if they keep going as they have been, they will never get out of the poverty trap and be able to retire. Diane complains that even though Chris has increased his income over the years they do not know where the money goes and they are living from day to day.

The outstanding amount on their credit cards was $5,000 last year and now they owe about $10,000. They only pay the minimum monthly payment to keep their credit cards open. They also have a $250,000 mortgage on their home after drawing down money to improve their home and buy a new car for Diane.

Apart from superannuation savings of $75,000, the couple does not have any other savings and they believe their home mortgage will be there even when they can claim an age pension at age 67. Diane and Chris complain that they cannot keep going as they have been – they must find a way to pay off their mortgage before they retire otherwise they will be forced to sell their home, and then where will they live?

This story is common to some people who constantly live in debt without having any idea where their money goes.

After we discussed their financial problems with them we got Diane and Chris to write down three things they would like to achieve by the end of one year and to set priorities and timeframes in which they would achieve these targets.

Their targets were to:

— Start to keep track of everything the family spent in a notebook so they could identify excessive expenditure

— Reduce the credit card debt as fast as possible

— Draw up a budget by the end of the year to help them see how they could reduce the outstanding mortgage and increase their retirement savings.

After a couple of months of keeping track of their spending, they start to realise where their money has been spent. This enabled them to control their money better and eliminate unnecessary expenditure and they reduced their overall expenditure substantially. Diane stopped buying clothes she didn't need and Chris had a can of beer when he arrived home instead of stopping at the pub and drinking several. There were numerous other small expenditure cuts they were able to make. They both still complain about the hassle of keeping records of their expenses, but now admit that they can see where they were spending excessively and they can control their expenses through budgeting.

They are working towards their short-term goal of eliminating their most expensive debt as fast as they can by paying additional amounts off their credit card debt. Their target is to achieve this within one year.

Once they have done this they have resolved to pay their credit card in full within the interest free period every month. Then they will draw up a long term budget that will include making additional superannuation contributions, reduce Chris's tax liability as well as making additional payments into their home mortgage. If they stick to this plan they will be debt free and have more accumulated superannuation by the time they retire.

If you want to eliminate debts, accumulate wealth and live comfortably then budgeting is the starting point of your journey.

You can see from Chris and Diane's story that simply having access to more money does not solve financial problems; they also needed to change their attitude towards managing their money. With a disciplined approach towards budgeting, families can help themselves and their children to understand the need to save little and often and invest wisely to create wealth for retirement.

KEEPING YOUR BUDGETING ON TRACK

We all have 'needs' and 'wants' that we would like to satisfy in life. The needs are the basic things that are required to live a healthy and comfortable life (for example, housing, food, clothing, transportation, electricity and gas, clean water, basic education, health, etc). On the other hand, wants are the things that each of us would like to have in order to improve our quality and enjoyment of life. These vary from person to person, but may include eating out in restaurants, holidays, jewellery, fashionable clothing, an expensive car, an up-to-the-minute entertainment system, money to finance an enjoyable hobby and so on.

Ask yourself before spending your money on something "do I need or want it?" If you can do without that item and if by buying it you would be delaying your early retirement, then you should defer buying it to a later date. Better still convince yourself not to buy it at all.

Setting targets

Before you start your budget list three things that you would like to achieve by the end of one year and set timeframes in which you will achieve these targets. This enables you to think about the cost of each target, and think about which of your targets is the most important for you to achieve. Having prioritised targets will give you an incentive to stick to your plan.

Your targets may be quite different from those of Diane and Chris. For example it may be paying for various items as shown in the following table.

Table 4.1 Short term targets

My target/goal	Total money needed	When to achieve	Priority
Buy a new dishwasher	$1,200	As soon as possible	1
Take a holiday	$1,800	After 6 months	2
Save money and invest for early retirement	$10,000	Within 12 months	3
Total needed to achieve all goals	**$13,000**		

Practical steps to budgeting for success

You may feel that it is too early or too difficult to set up and maintain a budget especially for your early retirement plan. However, if you fail to identify and address any financial problems you currently have through careful budgeting you will almost certainly find that those problems will grow over time. So, if you want to retire early now is the time to start using these simple steps. Don't fall into the trap of relying on memory or estimates as you will miss too many items.

STEP 1 Gather all the information you have about your income over the past 12 months, such as your pay slips or annual payment summary, and details of other income such as interest and dividends (you may already have the information about your income recorded in your tax return). You will also need details of expenditure you have incurred which you can identify from the bills you have paid, receipts you have, bank statements, credit card statements and cash you have withdrawn and spent. This will mean that the figures you include in your budget are going to be based on what you have *actually* spent.

STEP 2 Keep a diary for two weeks or a month and record everything you spend. This will include things like buying food, buying a coffee and cake in a coffee shop with a friend, eating out, buying a magazine that catches your eye, buying chocolates and alcohol, the money you give to your children, making donations and paying for medical expenses. This will give you a good idea of where your money is going, and also alert you to any unnecessary expenditure, thereby giving you money you could save to meet your target.

STEP 3 Start to draw up your budget. You can either do this here in the form provided in this book or if you have even a basic knowledge of a computer program such as Microsoft Excel you can customise it to suit your circumstances in a spreadsheet using our form as a guide.

STEP 4 Review and manage your budget on an ongoing basis. This is the most important part of your financial management plan. Your budget should be flexible enough to cope with unexpected expenses. For example, if you need money to meet an emergency modify your budget so that your cash flow remains positive. Make sure that you keep your budget as simple as possible. Whatever budgeting system works for you is fine – just make sure you stick to it.

MAKING YOUR BUDGET WORK

Unless you base your budget on actual facts it will not work. Major sections of a budget include:

— Income

— Essential expenses

— Discretionary expenses

— Balance/savings capacity (net income less total expenditure).

Make sure your budget is a realistic and honest list of the income you are fairly certain of earning and of your actual spending, rather than what you would like to spend if only you didn't buy unnecessary things on the spur of the moment. The only person you are fooling with an overly optimistic budget that does not give a true picture of all of your spending is yourself and it is doomed to fail.

Starting on the first day of the month, keep a column in your diary, or buy a separate diary and keep it with you to write down everything that you spend each day, (right down to the cost of a postage stamp) and tally it up at the end of each week. For example:

Weekly cash expenditure

Food	$100
Lunches and coffees	$60
Entertainment	$65
Car expenses	$50
Magazine	$5
Total cash spent in one week	**$280**

This will give you a wake-up call of where your money is going and also help you to restrain your spending when you see how much you are spending each week.

If you find this too boring there is a less tedious approach and it can in fact be more accurate. Take a set amount of money with you each day, count the remaining money each evening before you go to bed and record the difference between what you started with and what you now have in your diary as that day's spending. Try to remember where it has gone and record any balance as sundries. If you find it hard to restrain your spending leave your credit card at home and only carry the cash you need. For example if you decide that you spend less than $20 each day, take only $20 with you.

You don't need to be too harsh or frugal with yourself. Your lifestyle should not be destroyed just because you are trying to stick to a budget. You are more likely to stick to your budget if you include an allowance for entertainment and a treat each week.

Once you have recorded cash expenditure for a week, transfer the total for the week to a monthly summary as follows:

Summary of weekly cash expenditure for the month 1

Cash expenditure week 1	$280
Cash expenditure week 2	$300
Cash expenditure week 3	$300
Cash expenditure week 4	$270
Remaining days in the month	$130
Cash expenditure for the month	**$1,280***

*Transfer this figure to the 'Monthly actual' column in Form 4.1 at the end of this chapter.

Recording your actual income and budgeted income

You can then start writing down your actual income and write up your budget now that you have gathered the information. To help you we have provided a form at the end of this chapter. This form allows you to write down your monthly budget and then compare it at the end of the month with the money you have actually spent. Any negative figures in the difference column will highlight where you have over-estimated your income or underestimated your expenditure. Carefully review your discretionary items and see which can be cut back or cut out to reduce your expenditure and increase your savings capacity further.

Once you have completed your monthly budget calculate your annual budgeted income and living expenses and any commitments or obligations you have each year.

Paying your pre-determined savings amount first

It is important to pay yourself first when you receive your income by putting a predetermined amount as savings aside for your early retirement. Then pay the bills and live on the remaining money. Remember superannuation savings alone may not be enough to provide you with the financial capacity to retire early, particularly if you encounter unforeseen circumstances along the way, such as ill health or an interruption to your career.

Getting your bills organised

Get into a routine of organising your bills when you receive them and pay them on time. Once you have paid your bills file them together in an organised way. If all else fails even a cardboard box is better than nothing. You will be able to locate information quickly if you use a separate clear plastic holder for different paid bills – for example put your paid electricity and gas bills in one, your telephone and internet bills in another, municipal and water rates in another, tax deductible items in another and so on. They will then all be sorted immediately saving you time at the end of the year or if you need to locate one of your bills for some other reason.

If you have problems paying bills quarterly try to pay them monthly (as long as you are not paying an additional charge for doing so). You can arrange to pay many bills and your mortgage directly from your bank account or credit card by entering into a direct debit arrangement. However, be careful, some banks charge a fee if you inadvertently overdraw your account. It is therefore important to make sure you organise the payments to come out of a bank account when you know there will be enough money available, for example after your salary goes into your account.

Another alternative is to get electronic bills that you then pay by credit card or from your bank account at a time of your choosing.

KEYS TO BUDGETING SUCCESS

A successful budget will be well planned, clear, realistic, flexible and family-friendly.

A well planned budget takes a bit of time to prepare and should be devised and accepted by all family members. If you think of your budget as your family's personal business and make it into a family activity by involving your family members, including any dependent children you have, you will all understand where it is coming from. Make it fun by having a brain-storming session on where the money is spent and how savings can be made and offer rewards for the money-saving ideas (staying up later for children for example). You will be surprised at what your children come up with. It may be as simple as turning the lights off when a room is not in use or making lunches at home or drinking water instead of soft drink. The value of all this is far greater than the budget, it is that your children will appreciate the costs involved in running a home and also learn how to manage money wisely and watch out for waste. If you are single and you want some ideas invite a couple of your friends over for a 'budget night'. Serve them an easy to prepare meal and get them to bring a bottle of wine, and then get them talking. Have a notebook at the ready to jot down good ideas, and make sure that you don't drink so much wine that you can't remember what was said the next day!

A good budget is realistic. If you buy takeaway food and want to continue to do so you must include it. It should allow you to save money while still enjoying your lifestyle. It has to be flexible too. Your income and expenses may change if your family or employment situation changes or you have unavoidable and unexpected expenses. This may require you to revisit your budget and revise it.

Always have some emergency money for any unanticipated events so that your budget and family will not suffer. You can reduce some of your discretionary expenditure to create a source for your emergency fund. Emergency events include someone in the family getting sick or having an accident or loss of a job or damage to your car or home. If you have a drawdown facility on your mortgage you can keep your emergency money in your mortgage. It will be there when you need it and at the same time reduce the interest you are paying on your outstanding loan when you don't.

CASE STUDY: Breadwinner and spender

A very successful businessman said that he tried to draw up a budget when he first married 30 years ago. He and his wife failed once and have never since been able to stick to a successful budget. Now he is the breadwinner and his wife is the financial spender. Over the years he has earned and she has spent millions of dollars but their wealth has not improved as it could have done due to poor budgeting.

The point of this case study is to remind you that, regardless of your level of income, to be financially successful you have to live within your budget by spending less than you earn.

It is important to revise it regularly when changes occur. You can use budgeting as an initial and essential step of achieving your financial goals that will lead to the ability to retire early.

Tips for successful budgeting

1. Set clear budgeting goals and stick to your budget by involving all family members.

2. Start saving at least 10 per cent of your gross income and invest wisely. When you receive a pay rise, save the increased amount and you will be amazed how much you will be saving for your retirement over the years.

3. If you have credit card debt and you are making minimum monthly payments rather than clearing your debt during the interest free period, pay it off as quickly as you can by paying more than the minimum balance each month. The interest charged on an outstanding credit card debt can be very expensive – up to about 20 per cent interest on your after-tax money. If you are in the highest marginal tax bracket the effective rate is almost 40 per cent interest!

4. Pay off your highest interest charging, non-tax deductible debts next, such as personal or hire purchase loans.

5. Pay off your home mortgage quickly by making regular fortnightly payments and additional payments.

6. Pay off your highest deductible interest loans.

7. Keep your expenses within your budget. Make sure to reward yourself occasionally by going out to a restaurant for dinner, or to the theatre or by taking a short holiday.

8. Pay your bills on time to avoid late penalty payments, fees and charges.

9. Look for sales and bargains by buying good quality items at bargain prices. Remember nobody is rich enough to buy cheap goods that do not last.

Form 4.1. Monthly budget

	Monthly budget $	Monthly actual $	Difference (+ or -)
GROSS INCOME			
Salary/wages			
Business income			
Interest received			
Dividends			
Rent received			
Other income			
Total income			
Less estimated tax payable			
Net income			
ESSENTIAL EXPENDITURE			
Food and other household expenses			
Clothing			
Electricity			
Gas			
Telephone and internet			
Education			
Rent/mortgage/rates			
Transport			
Vehicle			
Medical and dental costs			
Insurance			
Home			
Contents			
General			
Life			
Income protection			
Medical			

	Monthly budget $	Monthly actual $	Difference (+ or -)
Childcare/children's spending money	_____	_____	_____
Household help/repairs	_____	_____	_____
Total essential expenditure	_____	_____	_____

DISCRETIONARY SPENDING

Cash expenditure	_____	_____	_____
Entertainment	_____	_____	_____
Take-away food	_____	_____	_____
Alcohol, cigarettes and soft drink	_____	_____	_____
Personal care/grooming	_____	_____	_____
Hobbies and memberships	_____	_____	_____
Travel and holiday	_____	_____	_____
Gifts/donations	_____	_____	_____
Other*	_____	_____	_____
Total discretionary spending	_____	_____	_____
TOTAL EXPENDITURE	_____	_____	_____
BALANCE/SAVINGS CAPACITY = Net Income less Total Expenditure	_____	_____	_____

*Write further details here:

_____

_____

_____

_____

_____

_____

_____

Form 4.2 Annual budget planner

	Jan	Feb	Mar	Apr	May	Jun	July	Aug	Sep	Oct	Nov	Dec	Total
GROSS INCOME													
Salary/wages													
Business income													
Interest received													
Dividends													
Rent received													
Government receipts													
Other income													
Total income													
Less tax payable													
Net income													
ESSENTIAL EXPENDITURE													
Food and other household expenses													
Clothing													
Electricity													
Gas													

	Jan	Feb	Mar	Apr	May	Jun	July	Aug	Sep	Oct	Nov	Dec	Total
Telephone and internet													
Education													
Rent/mortgage/rates													
Transport													
Vehicle													
Insurance													
Home													
Contents													
General													
Life													
Income protection													
Medical													
Medical and dental costs													
Childcare/children's spending money													
Household help/repairs													
Total essential expenditure													

	Jan	Feb	Mar	Apr	May	Jun	July	Aug	Sep	Oct	Nov	Dec	Total
DISCRETIONARY SPENDING													
Cash expenditure													
Entertainment													
Take-away food													
Alcohol and soft drink													
Cigarettes													
Personal care/grooming													
Hobbies and memberships													
Travel and holiday													
Gifts/donations													
Other													
Total discretionary spending													
TOTAL EXPENDITURE													
SAVINGS CAPACITY													
= Net Income less Total Expenditure													

CHAPTER 5

What type of investor are you?

In this chapter you will learn about:
- Investor profiles
- Personal risk profiles
- Your investment return needs and objectives
- Investment time frames
- Investment cycles.

S ome people tend to think about investing for retirement either on an annual basis, (especially on new year's day, briefly as a new year's resolution) or shortly before retirement. This approach to retirement planning is not good enough if you want to retire early. You need to be more proactive and take an active role. You cannot afford to invest and then forget about your investments, whether in superannuation or other investment assets, as the investment world can be a real mine field. We have all witnessed recently just how markets can go down during financial crises and the effect this can have on our investments.

If you have taken the first steps on the road to financial freedom, put a budget in place and analysed your net worth, then now is time for your investment education. And the place to start is with YOU!

A financial plan for an early retirement should be built around your unique personal circumstances and preferences. Everybody's needs are different. There is no single investment portfolio that meets everyone's needs. So it is important to analyse your own personal investment philosophy before making any investment decisions. You will need to consider the following factors:

— Your investment profile
— Your personal risk profile or tolerance for risk
— Investment return needs and objectives
— The amount of money you have to invest
— Your investment time horizon
— Your tax position

Each of these factors is discussed in more detail below.

INVESTOR PROFILES

Your investor profile describes what kind of investor you are. You can use the scale from 1 to 10, 1 being a conservative investor, to 10, an aggressive investor. After considering all the information in this chapter you will have a good idea of where you sit on this scale. Once you have established which investor profile best suits you, you will better know in which investment sectors to invest. It could be that you are more suited to keeping a large proportion of your investments in cash and fixed interest or maybe you are more comfortable investing in the sharemarket or property markets. Also note that your profile may change at different stages of your investing journey. The next step will allow you to estimate how your investment portfolio will perform and the returns you might expect.

Conservative investor profile

If you are a conservative investor your primary concern is to preserve your capital to produce a reasonably stable stream of income with little or no opportunity for capital growth. This profile is common to many people approaching retirement and retired people. They are nervous that in order to obtain growth they need to invest in asset classes that are inherently more volatile in the shorter term, despite tending to perform much better in the longer term.

This profile is not risk free. In the longer term, without any assets growing in value, tax and inflation slowly erode your investments because the amount that the income can purchase is continually reducing. So more and more capital needs to be used up to maintain the same purchasing power. If you are retiring or already retired, you should still consider a mix of mainly income and some capital growth assets, such as shares which offer a good dividend yield and some growth potential. There can be tax benefits attached to sharemarket investments if the company's dividends are fully franked (this is discussed later in chapter 6).

Balanced investor profile

If you are a balanced investor you will be midway between a conservative investor and an investor who is aggressively seeking capital growth. You diversify your wealth into a variety of investments that give you both income and capital growth, in order to reduce the risk of poor returns and loss of capital value.

You still have the risk that your capital can fall in value but there is also the possibility of growth in the value of some of your assets. Your investments will be spread across all of the main asset classes, including equities, which are mainly Australian shares and fixed interest. You may also have a small percentage of international equities, mortgages, property trusts and real property.

Aggressive investor profile

If you are an aggressive investor your prime concern is to create capital growth to accumulate wealth by holding investments for five to seven years. This timeframe will allow you to ride the ups and downs of volatile markets. Buying good quality investments and holding them is one approach you can take to accumulate assets for your retirement. This type of investor usually has income from employment or business, is concerned with the after-tax return from investments and has a high tolerance to risk.

PERSONAL RISK PROFILE

Risk is simply the possibility that the investment will not perform as you expect or the chance of losing some or even all of your money in a particular investment. There is generally a trade off between investment return and risk. You do not have to take too much risk to accumulate wealth for your retirement provided that you stick to simple investment rules and start saving early. To invest successfully you need to have a sound mindset, discipline and a framework for making decisions.

It is very important to assess how much risk you are prepared to take before you invest your hard-earned money. Your previous investment experiences may affect how much risk you can tolerate to achieve a certain level of return on your investments.

You must also learn to control your emotions as investments go up and down in value. When an investment market, say, the sharemarket is going up in value, investors generally feel overly optimistic about the market's future and tend to make investments. However, share prices sometimes change very quickly and some people do not do their homework first before making investment decisions, instead they follow the herd and panic easily. Some people take too much risk while the market is going up and they panic and sell their investments at the worst time as the market goes down and they crystallise their losses. Fear and greed are the most prevailing emotions that need to be controlled to be able to make sound investment decisions.

If you invest in a market that you are not familiar with you will find that making money is more difficult than losing money. You need to understand and be comfortable with any investment you make and ensure that it matches your risk tolerance. If you are losing sleep over a particular investment then that investment is not for you. You should either find out more about it so that you feel more comfortable or try to get out as soon as is practicable. In the investment world, ignorance is not bliss, as there are many unethical people and market complexities.

Assess your tolerance for risk carefully so that you do not make panic decisions or sell your investments at the worst possible time. One of the best approaches to assess risk tolerance is to ask yourself whether you can accept a loss in the value of a particular investment and whether you could hold your investment even if it goes down in value. If you feel comfortable with a particular investment then it suits your risk tolerance.

Overall investor types are given in Table 5.1 below. Remember that your risk profile and investor type can change with time and investment experience.

Table 5.1 Classification of investors

Type of risk profile	Type of investment
LOW (Conservative)	Conservative investors choose low risk investments and are prepared for low returns with capital stable investments. There is little concern placed on the effects of tax and inflation on the return on investments. Most retired people may be classified as conservative investors. People with a low tolerance for risk can generally accept losses up to 5 per cent over a one year period. Suitable investments include term deposits, bonds and some property investments.
MEDIUM (Balanced)	Prudent investors choose a balanced portfolio to obtain capital growth by taking some investment risk in the medium to long term. Effects of taxation and inflation factors are taken into account in their investment strategy to achieve greater returns. People with a moderate tolerance to risk can generally accept losses of between 5 to 15 per cent over an annual period. Suitable investments include long term bonds, and blue chip, lower-risk, dividend-paying shares.

Type of risk profile	Type of investment
HIGH (Aggressive)	People with a high tolerance for risk can generally accept losses of between 15 to 40 per cent of capital over the short term to achieve potentially greater long term returns. Suitable investments include growth shares and shares in small firms. Wealth creation through greater capital growth with a diversified investment portfolio is the main objective of these investors. Security of capital is a secondary objective.

Of course, you can reduce your risk profile by investing your money into different investments so that you average your losses if a particular market goes down.

Look at this line and think about where you consider your investor profile falls:

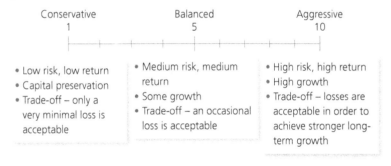

YOUR INVESTMENT RETURN NEEDS AND OBJECTIVES

Investment returns include income and/or capital growth and depending on your needs and personal circumstances you may prefer mainly capital growth or income. For example, if you are creating wealth for your early retirement, you may choose assets with capital growth and some income. Then later you may choose capital-secure, income-producing assets during your retirement years. Most people want a blend of income from dividends, rent or interest (which may come in the form of a distribution if you have invested in managed funds) and capital growth from their investments. This can be achieved with a carefully chosen mix of investments that includes property and shares.

It is important to bear in mind that there is generally a trade-off between income and growth. While you are setting up your investment portfolio make sure that you mix your investments in predetermined portions among carefully selected managed funds, and direct investments in shares, property and fixed interest.

Superannuation money accumulated during our working lives can range from a very small amount to millions of dollars. It will depend on how much of your income you can divert into saving and investment and then how effective your investment strategy proves. We discuss this in chapter 7. It is appropriate to remind you here that the more you can invest the better your chances of retiring earlier and with a more comfortable financial future. You need to build and retain sufficient capital to create wealth for you to be able retire when you choose. Then this capital must be able to generate a passive income that should be enough to sustain your desired lifestyle.

INVESTMENT TIME FRAMES

In retirement planning, the length of time you invest (your investment time horizon) can directly affect your ability to reduce risk in fluctuating investment markets. Your time frame is important when investing in a portfolio that comprises growth assets (specifically shares and property). As a rule of thumb, a minimum investment time horizon of at least five years should be chosen when investing in growth assets, but closely monitor your investments to minimise potential losses as prices go down.

You need to have a plan for entry, exit and position sizing for all of your investments. Timing the market is important but it is very difficult to successfully time your investments consistently. The main warning we can give you is don't enter the market when it is at an all-time high, because it is highly likely to experience a fall in value (referred to as a 'correction') in the near future. All market linked investments go through up and down cycles but when you hold good quality investments, time will smooth short term price fluctuations in the market. Of course you need to follow the performance of your investments carefully while you are holding them in your portfolio.

Completion of an investment cycle usually takes five to seven years. Investment cycles create buy or sell opportunities for savvy investors to make profits and others to make losses! For example, share prices for financial services may be falling while prices for industrial companies may be going up. Similarly, property prices can be increasing in one city while similar properties in another city may be dropping. Investment cycles or fluctuations generally become less important when you choose a long investment time frame.

If your investment time horizon is long you can take greater risks for greater potential return. Where you are investing to accumulate wealth for retirement and to have a regular income stream during retirement, your time horizon tends to be medium to long term. This period is usually between five to ten years. Holding investments longer than an economic cycle can reduce volatility risk.

Unless you are an active share trader, investing in the sharemarket should be viewed as a medium to long term option. Having said that, when you make a reasonable profit on your sharemarket investments you may choose to sell some of your shares to lock in the gains you have made. Remember nobody goes broke by taking profits, but look at your overall tax position and the tax you may need to pay before selling an asset and realising a capital gain.

In investment planning and portfolio management investments are mainly categorised into three groups; short term, medium term and long term.

1. **Short term (up to one year time frame).** Most short term investments are interest bearing investments with little or no capital growth and include bank term deposits, bonds and cash

management trusts. Short term investments are suitable for people who mainly require income and are not willing to accept price fluctuations of investments.

2. **Medium term (from three to five years).** Medium term investments allow investors to grow their capital in spite of some fluctuation in value over the investment term. Medium term investments include investments in shares, listed property trusts and bonds.

3. **Long term (more than five years).** Long term investments are used for both capital growth and income. This can be achieved by investing in shares, real estate and managed equity funds. Since the duration of the investment is spread over a longer period of time, the effect of price fluctuations and entry and exit costs are lower as they too are spread over a long period of time.

TAX POSITION

The most important part of investing for retirement is to maximise your after-tax returns. It is important to take into account the impact of tax on your investments. High dividend yielding shares can provide tax effective income if they are fully franked (that is, the dividends you receive have been taxed at the company rate of tax). Fully franked dividends reduce tax payable because a tax credit passes to you as an imputation credit. Even if you cannot use up all of these tax credits, you may get them refunded by the Australian Taxation Office (ATO).

If your marginal tax rate is higher than the company tax rate, then you will pay tax at your marginal tax rate less the company tax rate on fully franked dividends. This is attractive to high income earners. If your marginal tax rate is the same as, or lower than the company tax rate, franked dividends may offset the tax payable on other income with any surplus being refunded.

Capital growth is only taxable upon the sale or disposal of your investment. So high income earners may be wise to defer sale of these assets until they are in a lower tax bracket.

LIFECYCLE ISSUES

For many people, as they grow older their personal tolerance for risk changes. As they gain more investment experience and knowledge they can take calculated risks to accumulate more retirement wealth. Tolerance for risk then often reduces the closer to retirement they get. The following table illustrates these issues.

Table 5.2: Investment factors and lifecycles

| | | | Lifecycle | | |
Factor	Early years (20 to 30)	Middle career (30 to 40)	Late career (40 to 55)	Near retirement (55 +)	After retirement
Risk profile	High	High	High to moderate	Moderate	Low
Investment return needs	Growth	Growth	Growth	Income/ Growth	Income
Investment time horizon	Long term	Long term	Long to medium term	Medium term	Medium to short term
Tax Issues	Some importance	Very important	Very important	Very important	Some importance

This table shows how an investor's profile and needs may change over life. Protecting your capital should be taken into account at every stage of your life. You tend to take fewer risks at retirement and tax issues may lose some of their importance.

Over a lifetime we all face many changes that impact on our ability to create wealth and plan for our retirement. The following factors play an important part in establishing our risk profile, investment return needs, investing time horizon and taxation issues:

— Changes in career and employment situation, including changing jobs, redundancy, unemployment

— Changes in family circumstances such as marriage, a new child in the family, divorce and death

— Changes in economic and market conditions such as recession.

An understanding of the various aspects of your investment profile will allow you to assess that proper balance in building wealth for retirement and retirement planning.

INVESTMENT CYCLES

We have already touched upon investment cycles in our discussion on investment time frames. Now we look more closely at cycles. Every investor needs a basic understanding of economic cycles as they affect the important issue of timing your investment purchase and sale decisions.

Investment cycles and economic conditions are closely linked. The economy moves through different cycles from boom to recession, depression, recovery and back to boom again as shown in Figure 5.1 below. Economic cycles can last on average seven years or so. As an educated investor it is important to accept those cycles and make the most of them since they can create buying and selling opportunities.

Fig. 5.1 Economic cycles

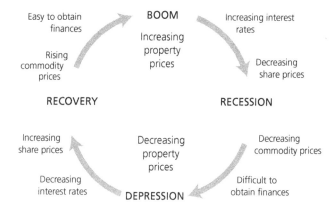

It is important to recognise that cycles can affect sections of asset classes differently. For example, property prices in one city or area may be going up, while similar properties in another city or area may be stable. Or share prices for mining companies may be falling in value while prices for companies in the financial services industry (banks, insurance companies, etc.) may be experiencing a boom.

INVESTMENT TIMING

If you are an active investor then you may buy certain shares or property when prices go down and sell when the prices reach high levels. For most investors though, particularly in the context of retirement planning, a buy and hold strategy is more suitable. If you buy good quality assets at low or reasonable prices and hold them, then the value of your investments should go up over time.

Buying and holding good quality investments removes short term price fluctuations. If your investment strategy is a long term one, then these cycles or fluctuations have less impact. The main thing is not to panic when the market goes down. This happens frequently in the sharemarket.

You should develop entry and exit strategies for your investments before you make investment decisions and stick to your plan. Think carefully before holding investments that are rapidly going down in value by putting a stop loss strategy in place. Some investors lose substantial profits when they stay in the market too long. Remember you will not go broke selling an investment and realising a profit. Set benchmark return and loss levels of say 25 per cent then as soon as the price drops by 25 per cent sell that asset to minimise your losses. A similar approach can be applied to gains.

If you do not want to get involved in timing the market for making investment decisions, you can invest into managed funds. This is a passive investment style and it may suit some investors who do not have sufficient time or knowledge to manage their investment portfolios or those with a more conservative investor profile.

CHAPTER 6

Investment basics

In this chapter you will learn about:

- Retirement investment risks
- Return on your investments
- Types of investments for retirement
- Shares
- Property
- Managed investments
- Gearing
- Common mistakes to avoid in investing.

Now that you are aware of your investor type and how you can cope with risk, the next step on your financial retirement journey is to consider all the investment options open to you. The investments you select and how well you manage them can have considerable impact on your nest-egg and how long it lasts during your retirement.

RETIREMENT INVESTMENT RISKS

Selecting an investment is as important as how long to keep it and when to sell it. Therefore we suggest that you regularly monitor your investment portfolio to find out whether it is at risk. There are several types of risk involved in any retirement investment decision. Almost all investments carry a different degree of risk and therefore any investment decision needs to be made after careful homework. We discuss the investment risks below.

Investment return risk

This is the risk of losing part or all of your money or the likelihood that your investment will not deliver its anticipated return. If your investment is sound and you make your investment decision after sufficient homework, you should be able to reduce your investment risk. In reality many people tend to invest as the market is going up or is close to its peak. This can create additional investment risk for those investors.

Investment risk can be reduced by diversification and sticking to your investment plan and investment time frame. The value of an investment can quickly fall and rise, especially in the sharemarket, due to various economic events, politics, wars, terrorism, etc. Therefore it is important to stick to your longer term objectives despite short term price fluctuations. Some investors panic when the prices fall and sell their investments to realise their losses. If the investment is a quality one and your investment strategy is to buy and hold then its value should go up over time. If you are trader rather than a buy-and-hold type investor then stick to your trading system and plan when making decisions with your share investments.

Market risk

All investments are subject to market risk and it cannot be eliminated altogether, even by diversifying your money into different investments or in more than one market. As a market goes through its periodic cycle of boom and recession, you need to make informed investment decisions to protect and grow your investments for your retirement. Your investments will always be affected by changes in interest rates, economic downturns, the state of the economy, sharemarket downturns, and property booms and busts. Your challenge is to weather these market environments as best you can to create wealth over the long term.

Business risk

Before you invest your money into a listed company, assess its fundamentals and the expertise of those who are managing that company and the directors' remuneration plans. Poor management, employee problems and resource management are some examples of business risks. Whatever you do, do not fall in love with a company because a company does not generally have any loyalty to you as a shareholder. It is very difficult to know what is happening at the company board level. By keeping up with the business media you can stay informed of much of the financial news. If you read about company directors being paid vast amounts of money when their company is making a loss, perhaps it is time to review your holding.

Legislative risk

Taxation and superannuation laws change often and these can affect your investment decisions and after-tax returns on your investments. If for example, dividend imputation rules are changed then your franked dividends may be less tax effective. With retirement income streams, any changes in taxation or superannuation rules could be very important. At time of writing when you convert your superannuation savings into an account based income stream at retirement, you are provided with a very tax effective structure. If the government changes the law and taxes the superannuation fund or the income stream then it would lose its tax attractiveness for retirees.

In order to make the most from changes in legislation you should consult with a competent accountant or superannuation specialist.

RETURN ON YOUR INVESTMENTS

The returns your investments generate play an important part in your retirement planning. The higher your returns the quicker you will achieve your goal of an earlier, financially secure retirement.

Returns from investments can be either income (such as dividends on shares or rent from property) or growth in the capital value of the investment, or a combination of some income and growth. Property and share investments can provide both income and capital growth. Therefore these investments are an important part of a portfolio for both pre-retirees and retirees.

Income-only investments are called debt instruments since you lend your money to a financial institution or to the government. Income-producing investments include government bonds, term deposits, cash management trusts and debentures. These do not provide any capital growth, but government bonds do have the potential for capital profit if interest rates fall during the term.

Shares and property can be owned either directly or through unit trusts or insurance bonds. These assets are primarily capital growth generating investments and they also provide income returns. As a rule of thumb, dividend yield or rental income of around 5 to 7 per cent and with the prospect of reasonable capital growth would be a good investment for most retirees and those investors with a balanced profile accumulating wealth for retirement.

Residential and commercial properties can provide both income and capital growth. An investment property usually increases in value over time while tenants pay rental which also increases over time.

Risk versus return

In general the risk and return on your investments are related. The risks include all of the risks discussed above and can result in anything from simple price fluctuations to the possibility of losing all of your money. An investment, the value and returns of which go up and down often, is more volatile and is said to be riskier than one which generates stable returns over time. For example, cash is regarded as low-risk and stable and shares as generally more volatile in the short term.

As you are getting closer to your retirement, you should choose to invest your savings into more stable investments to retain your invested capital. It is important that your money be invested in a way consistent with the level of risk acceptable to you.

TYPES OF INVESTMENTS FOR RETIREMENT

An appropriate investment strategy should meet your retirement objectives and needs by choosing investment options in cash, fixed interest, equities and property. Retirement investments can take the form of direct investment and managed investments. Superannuation money can be invested into asset classes that are suitable for your retirement needs and asset proportions can change over time depending on overall economic conditions.

Table 6.1 gives some guidance to the proportion of funds you should allocate to each asset class, depending on your investor type.

Table 6.1: Type of portfolios for different investors

Type of asset	Type of investor		
	Conservative	Balanced	Aggressive
Cash	50-70%	10-20%	5-10%
Fixed interest	30-40%	20-25%	10-20%
Australian Equities	0-5%	30-40%	40-50%
Property	5-10%	20-30%	15-20%
International Equities	0-5%	5-10%	10-25%

When you select investments for your retirement savings especially superannuation savings take into account the risk and return from a particular investment and other factors such as transaction costs, accessibility to the capital invested and liquidity. The following table summarises different investment types and their accessibility and liquidity.

Table 6.2. Factors affecting selection of an investment for retirement

Investment class	Return	Risk	Liquidity	Ease of entry/ access	Invest-ment costs	Time frame	Tax benefits
Cash	Lower	Lower	High	High/High	Low	Short term	Poor
Fixed interest	Lower	Lower	Mod	High/ Moderate	Low	Short to medium term	Poor
Shares	Higher	Higher	High	High/ High	Low/ Moderate	Short to long term	Good
Managed Funds	Higher	Higher	High	High/ High	Low/ Moderate	Short to long term	Good
Property	Moderate	Moderate	Low	Low/ Low	Very High	Long term	Good

Transaction costs include brokerage or agent fees, commissions, stamp duty, entry/exit fees and other costs and these vary with the type of investment.

Diversification is the most effective way to reduce risk when you invest your retirement savings. It involves spreading your money into several companys' shares, property, fixed interest and cash. Diversifying your retirement savings is desirable unless the amount of money for investment is relatively small and/or you are only investing for a short period of time. Some investors invest small amounts of money into many different assets to achieve diversification and in fact this can be a very ineffective way of spreading risk. Diversification requires periodic reviews of your portfolio, preferably annual reviews. As a rule of thumb, we suggest that 10 to 15 shares across different industry groups would provide enough diversification along with investments into property and fixed interest.

To sum up, long term investing in good quality assets generally improves returns and reduces overall volatility in your investment portfolio. However over-diversification can result in loss of control in managing the portfolio and incurs additional transaction costs. Keeping your investment portfolio simple will also save money on tax return preparation and accounting fees.

DIRECT INVESTMENTS

There are broadly two ways to invest and they are not mutually exclusive. Let's look at direct investment first. Direct investment provides ownership of assets to the investor and can be classified mainly in four groups:

1. Lifestyle investments
2. Fixed interest investments
3. Shares
4. Property.

Each of these is discussed briefly below.

Lifestyle investments

Lifestyle assets are mainly acquired to enhance your standard of living rather than contribute to wealth accumulation but some, such as collectables, antiques, your family home and holiday home can also increase your wealth. Examples of lifestyle assets that generally decrease in value include your furniture, car, boat, etc. If you move into a smaller home or retirement village unit when you retire the surplus from the sale of your home can provide additional money to fund your retirement.

Fixed interest investments

Fixed interest investments include term deposits, bonds and debentures, which pay defined interest payments for a specified period. The original investment is returned to the investor at the date of maturity. Both cash and fixed interest investments are debt investments. Fixed interest investments are suitable for short to medium term investing to provide moderate liquidity with fixed income returns. These investments are generally considered to be conservative and safe with low volatility. At retirement some people invest part of their savings into fixed interest accounts in order to receive regular interest income.

Fixed interest investments do not provide protection against inflation because the capital growth is nil.

Companies and governments raise money by issuing bonds (or other debt instruments) to a public market. Bonds are fixed interest securities and you receive interest as coupon payments and your principal at maturity. A bond is characterised by its face value, coupon rate, maturity and issuer.

The relationship of yield to price can be summarised as follows: when the price goes up, the yield goes down. When interest rates rise, the price of bonds in the market falls and vice versa. Bonds can provide diversification in your portfolio and a fixed income during retirement without risking your principal.

There is generally less risk in owning bonds than in owning shares in listed companies, but this comes at the cost of a lower return. Your bond investment's security depends on the bond issuer's ability to pay your principal and interest back. Therefore government bonds tend to be far more secure than those of a corporation. To select good quality corporate bonds check out the bond rating system that determines a company's credit risk. Table 6.3 shows the different bond rating scales.

Table 6.3 Bond credit ratings

S&P	Moody's	Credit worthiness – definitions
AAA	Aaa	**Prime.** Best quality bonds. They have the lowest investment risk. Interest payments are protected and principal is secure.
AA	Aa	**High Grade.**
A	A	**Upper Medium Grade.** They provide adequate security to principal and interest.
BBB	Baa	**Medium Grade.** Interest payments and principal security appear adequate for the present but can be speculative.
BB, B	Ba, B	**Speculative.** They are junk bonds with moderate protection of interest and principal payments.

S&P	Moody's	Credit worthiness – definitions
CCC, CC	Caa, Ca	**Extremely Speculative.** These junk bonds represent obligations which are speculative in a high degree.
D	C	**May be in Default.** These are junk bonds.

Warning: If the ratings agencies are paid for their work by the bond issuers for whom they issue those ratings, you need to be careful about their ratings' validity.

Shares

While you are accumulating wealth until retirement age we suggest that some of your money should be invested in shares (also referred to as equities).

Share investments are suitable for medium to long term investors to provide an opportunity for you to own a part of a listed company as a shareholder. They generally have high liquidity, (i.e. they can be bought and sold easily), with potential for capital gains and losses and usually provide a dividend income. Company performance, economic conditions and market sentiment can cause large fluctuations in value. However, you can spread your risk by diversifying across a number of shares in different sectors and even from overseas. Shares give an excellent opportunity to generate both income and capital growth that will create wealth for your retirement. You can use shares in your superannuation fund while accumulating funds and also they can be effectively used in an account based income stream.

There are two types of shares that you need to be aware of. The majority of shares listed on the Australian Securities Exchange (ASX) are ordinary shares. Ordinary shareholders receive part of the listed company's profit as a dividend which will vary with the performance of the company. The market value of an ordinary share is determined by demand from buyers and supply from sellers driven by other factors such as the performance of an industry sector, market sentiment, and local and overseas economic factors.

Listed companies mainly issue ordinary shares but some companies issue both ordinary and preference shares. Preference shareholders are generally entitled to a fixed rate of dividend which is paid before any dividend is distributed to ordinary shareholders. Preference shares may also be redeemable at a stipulated price at maturity or convertible to ordinary shares at a specified date.

Property

Individual property investment (residential or commercial) is considered a long term investment that (usually) generates a regular rental income and has capital growth potential. Whilst property investments provide low liquidity with high transaction costs, they can provide leveraging opportunities through gearing (borrowing part of the purchase price) to create wealth. Real estate can be used as security against which you can borrow to invest into other capital growth assets well before retirement. In addition, property can be a good regular income source at retirement.

An alternative to investing directly in property is to purchase units in listed property trusts. These are investments with medium to long term capital growth potential and they are also an income producing investment. Listed property trusts can provide diversification into the property market using less capital than a direct investment. However, check that the trusts you select are not heavily geared. Their level of borrowings should not be too high otherwise they are a high risk investment.

INVESTMENT PROPERTY

Real estate comprises land and the building structures attached to that land. Investment property can be residential houses, units and flats, commercial offices and shops and industrial factories. The selection of these investment properties is effectively determined by your income and capital growth requirements. Commercial offices and shops generally provide higher income return than other types of real estate investments but they can be more risky to rent, especially when the economy is in recession.

Benchmark net income returns are about:

— 5 to 9 per cent per annum from commercial property

— 2 to 5 per cent per annum from a residential property.

These return figures vary according to the property's location, size and position and the capital growth expectation from that property.

Overall, real estate investments should be accepted as long-term investments which can fluctuate in value, but which have historically increased in value over time above inflation. Property prices are affected by supply and demand and the level of interest rates and inflation.

If you manage your own superannuation fund it can purchase property investments if you have sufficient money in your fund to acquire the property without borrowing.

There are several risks attached to real estate investing including:

— Large sums of money are required to invest directly in real estate. A careful study of the market and property is required because of the potential for significant capital losses.

— There are high costs involved in buying and selling real estate reducing the potential return on the invested capital. Generally the cost of buying and selling is about 10 per cent of purchase and selling price. When you purchase real estate there is a large sum of stamp duty payable (and possibly GST on commercial properties).

— Buying and selling can take several months depending on the location of the property and demand.

— There may be extended periods of vacancies which, together with land tax, can reduce the real return on a real estate investment.

— Increasing interest rates and/or maintenance costs may increase real estate expenses and reduce your return.

— Devaluation of the property due to rezonings, nearby construction, etc.

— The property cannot be partially sold, meaning that upon sale the capital gain is taxed in full in one year.

MANAGED INVESTMENTS

If you do not follow the investment market regularly due to limited time or expertise and therefore do not feel confident in making your own direct investment decisions, managed investments can provide you with an alternative. They allow professional investment managers to make investment decisions for you. You can achieve diversification by pooling your money with that of the other investors in collective investments such as unit trusts, insurance investments, pooled superannuation trusts or annuities. Managed funds offer an alternative way to invest in equities, fixed interest or property markets for some investors.

You can improve potential earnings from managed funds by spreading your money across a range of asset classes, geographic regions and investment managers. For example, instead of purchasing shares in five companies directly for an outlay of $50,000, you could invest the money in an equity trust and have a share in 10 to 30 companies.

Before making any investment decisions in managed investments, be aware of entry, exit and ongoing fees and charges that you will incur. These fees are charged regardless of whether your investment goes up or down in value. Entry and exit charges can be as high as 5 per cent and ongoing management fees can be around 2 per cent per annum of your investment.

Advantages and disadvantages of managed funds

Managed investments can still be attractive to investors who have knowledge of the markets and experience in analysing investments. Some of the advantages of managed investments include:

— Professional management of the fund's portfolio

— Greater diversification achieved in each fund

— Reduced transaction costs

— Greater liquidity than some direct investments for accessing funds for disposal

— Regular investor reports and annual taxation statements prepared by experts and specialists.

On the other hand, direct investments allow investors to make decisions directly in buying and selling investments in their portfolio as the value of assets change in the market.

Capital secure or guaranteed investments

Whilst capital guaranteed investments guarantee that your original investment value will remain the same, capital secure investments can only offer security of capital invested. These investments are mostly offered by banks, friendly and life offices and they mainly invest in highly secure investments such as government and semi-government bonds and fixed interest securities. The return from these investments may not be as high as market linked investments.

Market linked investments

Market linked investment products are more volatile due to their exposure to equity markets. In the medium to long term, performance of these investments can be expected to exceed the capital secure and guaranteed investments.

Types of managed investments

You have a choice of listed and unlisted trusts. Listed trusts are traded on the ASX and their unit prices depend on supply and demand driven by the earning potential of the listed trust. Similar to listed shares, there are only a fixed number of units available.

Unlisted trusts are purchased or sold through the manager of the fund. The price of units is based on the trust's net worth after taking into account administration fees. The frequency of unit price valuation depends on the type of the trust. For example, equity trusts can be valued daily or weekly while property trusts may be valued semi-annually. Cash management trusts pay variable interest on a daily or weekly basis to reflect the market rate less the management fee levied.

Liquidity of unlisted trusts can be a concern when the market goes down for an extended period of time. The manager may restrict or stop redemptions and therefore investors' monies remain locked in them.

A unit trust is an investment vehicle consisting of a pool of money invested by many investors who own the units of that trust. The unit-holders have full rights to the trust's profit and capital in proportion to their investments. The trust is managed by a professional manager within a trust structure in which there are three components:

1. A trustee to ensure the legal operation of the fund is in compliance with its trust deed

2. A professional manager of the fund and its portfolio

3. Unit holders (investors) who purchase units in the trust to receive income and capital growth from the trust's assets.

Unit trusts are formed with different investment objectives. Some of the types of unit trusts are:

— **Cash management trusts:** These mainly invest in the short term money market and government backed securities to provide interest income with easy access to funds, in a manner similar to bank accounts. Capital growth is not provided and there are no taxation benefits since the income is fully taxable.

— **Bond trusts:** Invest in interest paying bonds which are issued or guaranteed by the commonwealth, state or local government, or semi-government bodies. Interest rates affect the value of assets since the bond price is inversely proportional to the interest rate.

— **Mortgage trusts:** These are often promoted as relatively secure, low risk investments. Investments are mainly made in larger mortgages and money is lent to property owners at a fixed interest rate to provide regular income to investors. However during the global financial crisis income and redemptions from some mortgage trusts were suspended due to mortgage defaults and where property prices had fallen capital losses occurred.

— **Equity trusts:** Mainly invest in the sharemarket and can be volatile due to the price fluctuations of shares. They are relatively liquid, and can provide dividend income and capital growth.

— **Property trusts:** Listed or unlisted property trusts allow indirect investment into the property markets, including investing in commercial, industrial and retail property. Listed property trust unit prices fluctuate similarly to share prices due to economic reasons. You should be aware that many such trusts that were highly geared fell dramatically in price during the global financial crisis and distributions were reduced or suspended.

INSURANCE BONDS

These are generally unitised investments and have a nominal term of 10 years. Insurance bonds are offered by insurance companies and are basically portfolio investments which include interest-bearing investments, equities or balanced portfolios. Similar to unit trusts, the performance of the insurance bond depends on the performance of the underlying assets in the portfolio. This investment involves a single premium life insurance plan to which annual bonuses are added at the end of each financial year.

Investors pay an initial premium in an insurance bond but it does not provide any income until it is redeemed. Any earnings are taxed at 30 per cent within the fund and reinvested into the fund. Investors can also make contributions to the bond of up to 125 per cent of the previous year's contributions without starting a new policy.

A nominated beneficiary can receive the proceeds of the investment in the event of the death of the investor. There is no tax liability on proceeds in the hands of the beneficiary, even if the death occurs within 10 years of the investment.

INTERNATIONAL INVESTMENTS

International investments can provide diversification in an investors' portfolio and spread risk across countries. However, currency fluctuations – especially where the overseas' currency falls against the Australian dollar – and lack of first-hand knowledge about the market, may deter some investors from investing internationally. International equity funds or investment trusts managed by fund managers can provide an option to diversify into international markets. International investments can be suitable for investors who are experienced and accept higher risks for higher potential returns.

GEARING

The Australian taxation system is punitive to higher income earners who pay almost half of their income in tax on income over a certain level. Gearing is popular financial jargon which is used often, but is less often understood. It is applied to the purchase of shares under a margin lending arrangement or investment properties purchased mainly with borrowed money.

Where you borrow money to invest in an asset that produces assessable income, and the income generated by this asset is less than the interest and expenses payable on the loan, it is called negative gearing. Under current taxation legislation, this shortfall may be claimed as a deduction against other taxable income to reduce your overall tax liability. If the value of your investment increases over time by more than the additional outlay to cover the after-tax cost of the shortfall between the rent that you receive and the interest you pay, your retirement savings will increase.

Negative gearing can be used as a tax planning tool to reduce tax payable when accumulating wealth for retirement. It can be a good strategy to build wealth for an early retirement. However, negative gearing can result in substantial financial losses upon a forced disposal of assets if the market value of your asset goes down. A gearing strategy can be useful if there is extra income from other sources to ensure your cash flow remains positive. Let's take a look at a couple of examples.

Example 1: Gearing when there is a capital gain. Margaret has $50,000 and she decides to borrow another $50,000 to invest the total ($100,000) in an income-producing growth share portfolio. The value of her investment portfolio increased by 10 per cent to $110,000 within 12 months. If she hadn't borrowed money, the 10 per cent return would apply only to the original capital of $50,000; the gain would have been $5,000. With the additional borrowed money the gain would be $10,000, less the cost of interest she has paid, so the gearing strategy has increased her return.

Example 2: Gearing when there is a capital loss. Assume that Margaret's investment had lost 10 per cent of its value rather than gained 10 per cent. Her investment portfolio would be worth $90,000, and there is still a $50,000 loan in place. This results in a net asset value of only $40,000.

A 10 per cent loss, therefore, has been doubled (i.e. $10,000/$50,000) with a net loss of $10,000. Plus she still has to pay interest on the $50,000 loan.

Income level

You need to have regular income from secure employment with proper income and disability insurance cover in place before you embark on a gearing strategy. Negative gearing is mainly suitable for investors who have high taxable income and are paying personal tax at the highest marginal rate because it helps them to reduce their tax liability while accumulating growth assets.

Aim to achieve a neutral or positive gearing position as soon as you can so that should you lose your job or become disabled, your investment can still pay the interest and other expenses.

Interest rates

Borrowing costs increase with the level of interest rates and the amount of borrowed money. When borrowing money to invest you should check whether you can service the loan if interest rates increase say by 3 to 5 per cent or more on investment loans during the period of the planned investment. It is better to be conservative than optimistic when it comes to borrowing money to invest, particularly when building assets for your retirement.

A margin loan that is highly leveraged can be a risky strategy as we all have witnessed over the last couple of years of the global financial crisis. It is not suitable for inexperienced investors and retirees who do not have sufficient cash to meet margin calls and interest payments. Margin lending assists wealth creation when the market value of investments is increasing but the reverse can occur if the market falls quickly. Then investors are faced with paying the margin call or having to sell their assets as the lender requires repayment of the loan.

Let's look at another case study that compares investing in shares using borrowed money and using your own money.

CASE STUDY: George and Mary's share portfolios

George and his sister Mary each owned a blue chip share portfolio valued at $60,000 which they had inherited from their parents.

After reading several websites which showed the benefits of borrowing money to invest Mary decided to accelerate her wealth by taking a margin loan with a limit of 70 per cent and interest payable at 8 per cent. Whilst Mary's maximum loan was $140,000 (calculated $60,000/(1 - 0.70) - $60,000), she decided her portfolio would be geared at no more than 60 per cent, that is $90,000 (calculated $60,000/(1 - 0.60) - $60,000). Her thinking was that this would protect her in the case of a fall in the market. She was very happy that she would own a portfolio worth $150,000 and get dividends based on the whole portfolio which would pay some of the interest on the loan plus she would get capital growth on the $150,000 portfolio.

She suggested to George that he should do the same, but George was cautious and didn't like the idea of borrowing money against shares. He stuck with the share portfolio he had inherited.

A year later a financial crisis resulted in the market value of the shares they each owned falling by 40 per cent.

Mary's shares fell in value to $90,000 and she received a margin call. Mary either had to find $36,000 cash immediately or the margin lender would sell her shares. Mary was unable to pay the margin call and so a domino effect meant that she ended up losing all of her share portfolio to pay the $90,000 loan.

George's portfolio fell in value by $24,000 to $36,000. However he did not have to sell any of the shares. He did not panic and kept his shares and over the next few months prices picked up again. His portfolio is almost back to $60,000 and he has received dividends all along so his retirement savings may have slowed, but they are still on track. Mary not only lost all of her shares, but also paid $7,200 interest.

The table below compares their results:

	George	Mary
Own capital invested	$60,000	$60,000
Margin loan	nil	$90,000
Total investment	$60,000	$150,000
Fall in investment	$24,000	$60,000
Value after 40 per cent fall in the market	$36,000	$90,000
Net proceeds after loan repaid	$36,000	nil
Interest paid at 8 per cent	nil	$7,200
Total loss	**$24,000**	**$67,200**

The moral of this story is that trying to get rich quickly by borrowing can result in losing all of your investment plus more in adverse market conditions.

Gearing magnifies the return on your investment while there is a gain in the portfolio. However, the losses are also magnified if the portfolio value decreases.

A gearing strategy should be considered while you have other income and are accumulating wealth well before retirement. It should generally be avoided once you have retired if you have little or no tax to pay and asset protection is paramount. The following issues must be taken into account before using a negative gearing strategy.

Never fully gear into the sharemarket. Gearing is only suitable for investors who can afford risk and have enough funds to pay any margin calls that can occur when share prices are going down. There is nothing wrong with getting wealthier over the long term without over-extending yourself with too much borrowing or leveraging!

MEZZANINE FINANCE

Mezzanine finance is a form of second mortgage. It ranks behind the first mortgage (which must be paid back first).

Developers use mezzanine financing to fund the difference between their developer's deposit (of say 5 to 20 per cent) and the amount banks will lend as a first mortgage on a building project (to, say, 50 to 60 per cent of the land value). Investors are paid a higher interest rate by the developer – usually 10 to 14 per cent – for a fixed period of time, in return for the greater risk of not having a first mortgage over the development. There may also be an additional payment to the investor when the capital is returned. However, if the developer runs out of money, mezzanine finance investors may lose all or part of their investment.

Although mezzanine finance promises to pay high fixed returns, it is important to check the details and the credentials of the organisation offering mezzanine finance and understand the risks involved. There should as a minimum be a second mortgage over the development as security (so that the mezzanine finance investors rank in front of ordinary creditors in the event of the project failing). The offer document should state that the funds must only be used for the particular project. Also investors should make sure that the return and maturity date is stated and fixed.

From an investor's point of view, mezzanine finance involves investing into projects and ventures financed outside the mainstream financial markets.

We do not consider that mezzanine finance is a safe investment as it involves disadvantages and risks – including that the investment is illiquid, the project may fall in value and mismanagement may cause a 'blow out' in costs or time – so if you do choose to invest some of your money in this way, only use a small percentage of available funds. In other words don't put all of your eggs in one basket. Make sure it fits into your investment strategy and risk profile and don't invest an amount that you can't afford to lose if the project does go bad.

Our opinion about mezzanine finance is, and always has been, that it is a high risk investment.

Our bad experience with mezzanine finance

Nearly all investors make a bad investment at some time and we are no exception. Despite our adverse opinion, we made an investment into mezzanine finance in late 2004 of an amount that fell within our investment strategy and risk profile. The information memorandum provided to us on the project stated it had 109 per cent in pre-sales (off-the-plan sales) (net) coverage of senior debt and mezzanine debt and security of the debt in the form of a second ranking mortgage over the property and a second ranking charge over the developer supported by a guarantee by Westpoint Corporation Pty Ltd and associated entities. The mezzanine finance would pay 12 per cent return per annum and we were told that the project was due to be completed within a year. On completion, the developer would repay the capital invested, together with an additional 2 per cent. So far we have only recovered about 22 per cent of the capital we invested.

COMMON MISTAKES TO AVOID IN INVESTING

Much of the information and advice about how to become effortlessly wealthy and successful is nonsense. Here is a list of seven common mistakes that successful investors should avoid:

1. **Staying in cash:** If your money is not invested over a period of time because you are afraid of the market your purchasing power slowly vanishes before your eyes.

2. **Following the herd:** Do not follow the herd by making investments in popular companies. An investment's future return can be inversely correlated to its current popularity. Most people invest their monies as the market peaks and end up as losers.

3. **Using lots of borrowings or leverage:** It is extremely difficult to consistently profit with margin loans in the sharemarket. There are two things against it. Firstly high interest rates can

apply. Secondly you are at the mercy of the market and if the share price falls you are forced to pay a margin call. If your margin account is 50 per cent leveraged, a 50 per cent drop in your portfolio can wipe out your wealth. During the global financial crisis, many portfolios with margin loans, even with high quality shares, lost a huge amount in value in very short periods of time.

4. **Lack of diversification:** Disaster can occur if your portfolio is too concentrated due to over-allocation in one area combined with over-confidence and a volatile market. Financial crises can decimate the values of even the best looking investments.

5. **Relying blindly on your adviser or broker:** Before you make any financial decisions, talk to your adviser or broker, then do your own homework and make your own decision. Advisers and brokers can have biases in advising you about specific investments, especially if commissions are involved.

6. **False sense of security:** Markets are not predictable and they do not care about investors. The most important objective of successful investors is not losing capital. Follow your investments carefully and do not hesitate to sell if you feel uncomfortable with them.

7. **Set and forget approach.** Remember a set-and-forget strategy in investment portfolios may not be the best approach. You always need to monitor your investments carefully.

Warning: if you are not comfortable or cannot understand any investment, do not invest into it even if it promises a good return. Remember, higher returns equal higher risks.

CHAPTER 7
The role of superannuation

In this chapter you will learn about:

- Why superannuation is so important
- Types of contributions
- How safe your superannuation is
- Different types of superannuation
- Superannuation funds' investment strategies
- Self managed superannuation funds
- Retirement funding with superannuation.

H
ave you taken the time to understand your superannuation and the types of investments you can make? Most people take little or no interest in their superannuation or how it is invested until they are close to retirement, or they actually retire. Then they are disappointed to find that their accumulated benefits are inadequate for their retirement needs. Other people who have their superannuation in a self managed superannuation fund, and have prudently managed it, will probably have increased their retirement savings over the long term, even if they lost money during the global financial crisis.

If you are one of those people who has not taken an interest in your super and you want to retire early it's time to wake up to the fact that your superannuation is a major part of your wealth. Other than your family home it is probably your largest investment and it will be able to provide you with a tax effective income stream, years before you are eligible to apply for an age pension. Therefore a full assessment of your superannuation is an important part of the early retirement planning process. Unfortunately you can't turn the clocks back, so you need to increase your superannuation savings as soon as possible.

If you haven't done so for some time, before you retire you should make the time to find out what you have in superannuation and how it may be taxed, or how tax can be deferred or even eliminated. Bear in mind that it may be too late once you retire because there may be fewer options open to you. For example, you can no longer salary sacrifice part of your salary or wages as superannuation. If you are over 65 you can no longer make any contributions to superannuation unless you work at least 40 hours in a 30 day period in the financial year before you make a contribution.

We have included a checklist (Form 7.1) at the end of this chapter that will help you to better understand the superannuation you have and as a result you will have better control of your superannuation money as you near retirement. If you or your employer is still contributing to your superannuation write down the details in the second form (Form 7.2). You may photocopy these forms.

WHY SUPERANNUATION IS SO IMPORTANT

Superannuation is one of the best ways to save tax effectively during your working life and build wealth for your retirement. Since this investment is generally not fully accessible until you retire at or after your preservation age or you reach 'retirement age' (which could be as late as age 67), you can watch your savings grow in value over time if you are careful in your selection of investments.

Your money in superannuation is invested over the long term, and can earn:

— Interest from money in a bank account
— Dividends from sharemarket investments
— Rent from money invested in real estate.

Your superannuation provider is set up as a trust fund or a Retirement Savings Account (RSA). Your fund invests your money and re-invests investment earnings for the benefit of all fund members. The combination of regular superannuation contributions and investment earnings after 15 per cent tax may allow these monies to grow to a large sum when you retire.

If you are an employee your employer is generally required to contribute into your fund at least 9 per cent of your ordinary wage or salary under the superannuation guarantee legislation or an industrial award if your income is $450 or more per month up to a capped amount. Income earned in the superannuation fund, plus concessional contributions it has received, are subject to 15 per cent tax.

Most Australians change jobs several times during their working lives. If you change your job, you may need to choose the fund that will hold your existing and future employer superannuation contributions. You can make a decision to rollover your superannuation benefits from your previous fund to your new employer's superannuation fund, to another superannuation provider or, if it is not preserved, you may decide to cash it in and retain it, or cash it and then reinvest it. If you have moved jobs a few times you may have superannuation benefits invested with several superannuation providers. If this is your situation, there may be advantages in consolidating your benefits into one superannuation fund. This makes your superannuation money easier to control and can result in you paying less fees and charges.

If you are interested in taking further control of your superannuation benefits you may consider setting up your own self managed superannuation fund. You can do this by yourself or with a total of up to four members. This can allow you greater flexibility in selecting and investing across different investment classes. However, you need to have a reasonable amount of accumulated superannuation and also to understand that there are costs involved in setting up this type of fund and ongoing administrative costs. We discuss self managed superannuation funds later in the chapter in the section on different types of superannuation.

Your superannuation builds up over the years as you or your employer continue to make contributions and the investments grow and benefit from compounding over the long term. When you reach your preservation age you can access part of your superannuation money each year as a 'transition to retirement account based income stream'. Once you retire or a condition of release is satisfied, the most common being reaching age 65, you can establish an account based income stream or withdraw the benefits as one or more lump sums of money. Retirement income streams and strategies relating to them are discussed in more detail in chapter 9.

Making contributions to superannuation can help you accumulate retirement wealth tax effectively while you are running your small business.

If you are self-employed (or live off your investments) you can choose your own superannuation fund and may be able to make tax deductible contributions. Deductible contributions are limited to the concessional contributions cap that applies to you. You can also make non-concessional contributions up to the non-concessional contributions cap. Contributions caps are included in the Appendix at the end of this book.

TYPES OF CONTRIBUTIONS

There are two types of contributions you can make into superannuation. These are called concessional contributions and non-concessional contributions. Both have indexed upper limits, called caps. We give details of the amounts of these caps in the Appendix at the end of this book. There are also penalties if you contribute too much superannuation in a financial year, (i.e. if you exceed these caps).

Concessional contributions

Concessional contributions are pre-tax contributions made by an employer or another person and include salary sacrifice and personal contributions which are being claimed as a personal tax deduction by a person eligible to do so. To be eligible to claim a personal tax deduction, up to 10 per cent of your earnings can come from an employer, including reportable fringe benefits and reportable superannuation contributions. In other words at least 90 per cent of your income must come from sources other than employment earnings and benefits. Let's take a look at an example.

Example: Claiming a deduction for personal contributions.
Jean is age 42 and she has the following income in the financial year:

Rent	$85,000
Interest	$15,000
Dividends, unfranked	$10,000
Personal contributions to superannuation	$25,000

As Jean does not have any employment income she can claim a deduction for concessional contributions of $25,000 as this amount is within her concessional contributions cap.

Your fund will pay tax (at 15 per cent at the time of writing) on concessional contributions it receives. However if you exceed your concessional contributions cap the excess contributions are subject to a further tax of 30 per cent plus the Medicare levy. The excess contributions count towards your non-concessional contributions cap. Your concessional contributions remain below the applicable cap.

Until 30 June 2012 there is an unindexed transitional concessional contributions cap of up to $50,000 for anyone age 50 or more who is permitted to receive or make such contributions. So if you turn 50 before that date, and you can afford to, you can take advantage of the higher cap.

Note that notional taxed contribution rates apply to calculate the concessional contributions amount for defined benefit members (more about defined benefits later in the chapter).

Non-concessional contributions

Non-concessional contributions are personal after-tax contributions. The cap is six times the concessional contributions cap for people under age 50 and is currently $150,000 in a financial year. If you are under age 65 you can contribute up to $450,000 at any time in a three year period.

If you are age 65 to 74 and you have satisfied the 40 hour in a 30 day period work test you can make non-concessional contributions of up to $150,000 in a financial year.

If your non-concessional contributions exceed these caps they will incur tax at the top marginal rate (45 per cent plus Medicare levy at the time of writing). It is therefore important to make sure that your non-concessional contributions do not exceed those caps.

Before converting your superannuation to an income stream

Remember that non-concessional contributions reduce your assessable income from your income stream whilst you are under age 60 and you will get a 15 per cent tax offset on the taxable part to reduce the tax payable on part of your income stream. Once you are age 60 or more all of your income stream from a taxed superannuation fund is tax free.

Restrictions on contributions

You can only contribute to superannuation after you reach age 65 if you satisfy the age and employment rules. If you are under age 65 there are no employment requirements and your fund can accept contributions up to the contributions cap. Let's have a look at some examples.

Example 1: Self funded retiree under age 65. Arthur, age 62, retired early and last worked 18 months ago. He receives a tax free superannuation income stream and substantial income from his investments. Arthur can continue to make contributions to superannuation whilst he is under age 65 and, because he does not have an employer who pays superannuation for him, he can claim a tax deduction for those contributions.

Example 2: Not working and age 65 or more on 1 July. Margaret has just turned 65 and is no longer working. Her fund can no longer accept superannuation contributions for her benefit.

Example 3: Working and age 65 or more but under 75. Geoff has just turned 65 and is still working for money for at least 40 hours in a 30 day period. He can continue to contribute to superannuation and the same tax rules apply to deductions and rebates if this work pattern continues, until he reaches age 75.

Even if you continue to work once you turn age 65, you have access to all of your superannuation benefits. You have the option to cash in some or all of your superannuation money at the same time as making contributions. Once you reach age 75 you cannot make any more contributions to your superannuation fund.

Salary sacrificing into your superannuation

In order to increase your retirement savings if you are an employee, a salary sacrificing arrangement can be entered into with your employer that will allow you to make superannuation contributions using your pre-tax income. If your income is above a certain level it will allow you to save income tax since superannuation contributions are taxed concessionally (15 per cent at the time of writing), whereas you pay tax at your marginal tax rate (see Appendix at the back of this book).

If your employer allows you to salary sacrifice part of your pre-tax salary into your superannuation fund you can reduce your taxable salary and make the additional contributions together with your employer contributions. Salary sacrificed superannuation contributions are reportable superannuation contributions. They are taxable in the fund and are added back to income tests to work out your entitlement to income tested tax offsets, certain commonwealth government payments made to people under age pension age, and the Commonwealth Senior Health Card. Since 1 January 2010 your employer's superannuation guarantee obligations have been based on your post-sacrifice salary. This means that your employer's superannuation guarantee obligation is reduced because the amounts sacrificed are treated as employer contributions.

If you are planning to salary sacrifice into superannuation make sure you are not giving up any employer contributions that would have been received as part of the superannuation guarantee system.

Example: Salary sacrifice unable to be claimed as a personal deduction.
Jeremy is age 47 and he has salary sacrificed $10,000 of his $20,000 wages into superannuation. His employer has continued to pay 9 per cent superannuation on $20,000.

He has the following income in the financial year:

Rent	$90,000
Interest	$5,000
Dividends, franked	$10,000
Wages	$10,000
Reportable superannuation contributions*	$10,900
	$125,900

*These include employer and salary sacrifice contributions that exceed his employer's obligatory superannuation guarantee contributions.

The superannuation guarantee contributions are excluded from reportable superannuation contributions and are limited to $900, being 9 per cent of the remaining $10,000 he receives as a wage. As his wages plus reportable superannuation contributions amount to $20,900, and this is more than 10 per cent of his total income, he cannot claim a deduction for any personal superannuation contributions.

SUPERANNUATION AND INSURANCE

Some industry superannuation funds have compulsory death and disablement insurance and some superannuation funds offer the option of purchasing life, disability and temporary incapacity insurance within the superannuation fund. A large superannuation fund pays lower insurance premiums on a group policy that is open to all the fund's members. If it is not compulsory and you require any of these insurances it is a more tax effective option than paying it from your own after-tax money, because you cannot claim personal tax deductions for the death and disability insurance premiums. On the other hand, your superannuation fund (including a self managed superannuation fund) can claim a tax deduction for these premiums against its other taxable income, including your employer's superannuation contributions and your personal contributions that you have claimed as a tax deduction.

PRESERVATION OF AND ACCESS TO SUPERANNUATION

Your super comprises preserved amounts (which remain in the superannuation system for your retirement) and non-preserved amounts (which you can access any time).

Since 1 July 1999, all superannuation contributions and investment earnings must be preserved in the superannuation system for your retirement. Except on very limited specified compassionate or severe financial hardship grounds, preservation rules prevent you from withdrawing your preserved superannuation benefits until you reach your preservation age and can satisfy at least one stipulated condition.

Your minimum preservation age depends on your date of birth. If you were born before July 1960 your preservation age is 55. If you were born after June 1964 your preservation age is 60. If you were born in between these dates you can find your preservation age in Table 7.1.

Table 7.1 Preservation ages

Your date of birth	Minimum preservation age
On or after 1 July 1964	60
July 1963 – June 1964	59
July 1962 – June 1963	58
July 1961 – June 1962	57
July 1960 – June 1961	56
On or before 30 June 1960	55

You can only withdraw preserved benefits from your superannuation account once you have reached your preservation age as a transition to retirement income stream until you also satisfy one or more of these 'conditions of release'. The conditions of release are:

— You have retired permanently from the workforce

— You have reached age 60 and subsequently left an employer who has made contributions for your benefit

— You have reached age 65

— You become disabled or die

— You hold an eligible temporary resident visa and permanently depart Australia

— You stop working for your employer and the value of your benefit is less than $200.

IS YOUR SUPERANNUATION SAFE?

Some people mistakenly think that they cannot lose their superannuation money. This is simply not true. Your superannuation should be prudently invested, but as with all market linked investments, it is only as safe as the type of investment choices you make.

The law does not guarantee your fund's investment value and earnings. These can rise and fall depending on market conditions and investment decisions. The higher the return your fund seeks, the greater the risk it takes of possible loss. On the other hand low risk investments, like money in a bank deposit, may produce low returns that do not make up for rises in the cost of living. Your superannuation trustee and their professional investment managers are paid to ensure the balance between risk and return is right.

If your superannuation has been invested in a careful way with a reputable superannuation provider, then it is generally safe, except that it may go down in value as the sharemarket, property or other sectors of investment markets go down. If you are given a choice of investments by your fund, some of these will give protection of your capital and others will not, so read the details of each choice carefully.

Every year millions of dollars of superannuation money are unclaimed or lost. You can check if you have any unclaimed super at ato.gov.au/super.

There are unscrupulous people in the community who want to defraud you of your hard earned money, and this includes your superannuation so be aware and take care.

TAKING CONTROL OF YOUR SUPERANNUATION

Unless there is a workplace agreement that requires your employer to pay your contributions to a particular industry fund, your employer contributes your superannuation contributions to your chosen fund. This can be your own self managed superannuation fund, or if you do not choose a fund, to a default fund chosen by the employer. Your decisions about your superannuation will affect how much money you accumulate for retirement. Depending on your workplace, you can control:

— Which superannuation fund you join – this occurs if your employer gives you a form offering you a choice of fund. If you do not make the choice your superannuation contributions will be paid to your employer's default fund.

— The type of investment strategy you choose for the contributions made to the fund.

— Whether to change to another fund if you are not happy with your existing fund.

— Whether to make additional personal superannuation contributions or salary sacrifice contributions.

— Whether you create your own self managed superannuation fund (SMSF) – this is a good option if you are a good money manager and investor and you have a substantial amount in superannuation already.

Unless your superannuation is in an SMSF, most investment decisions are made by the trustee of your superannuation fund with help from professional advisers and investment managers. Superannuation funds send an annual statement and fund report to each of the members. You may change your superannuation fund for various reasons and the most common reason would be changing jobs or if your fund is performing badly. If changing your fund is not possible or there are high exit penalties then you may be able to switch to a different investment strategy within the same fund. Any entry and exit fees are deducted from your superannuation savings and therefore it is important to check those fees and expenses before making a decision to switch funds.

DIFFERENT TYPES OF SUPERANNUATION BENEFITS

Superannuation benefit entitlements are most commonly accumulated benefits but if you work for a large company or a government department your entitlements may be defined benefits or a combination of both accumulated benefits and defined benefits. It is important that you know the type of benefits you are entitled to because each is different.

Accumulated benefits

Your superannuation is with an accumulated benefits superannuation provider if the annual statement shows total contributions for the year, plus earnings, less administration and other costs, and the dollar amount of the balance. This applies to most superannuation funds and all Retirement Savings Accounts (RSAs).

Contributions can comprise employer, salary sacrificed and personal contributions. In many ways an accumulation type fund operates like an ordinary bank account. Your accumulated benefit at any point in time is simply:

Accumulated contributions + Investment earnings – Fees and charges
– Taxes = Account balance

If you are a member of an accumulation fund contributions and earnings determine your final benefits. Therefore you bear the investment risk because if assets fall in value your account balance falls. On the other hand you get the benefit of rising asset values because your account balance increases.

Accumulated benefits are usually used where your superannuation benefits comprise contributions made:

— Under an industrial agreement or award
— To satisfy the superannuation guarantee requirements
— Because you chose to have additional superannuation paid either under a salary sacrifice arrangement or to make personal contributions.

Defined benefits

A defined benefits superannuation fund is one with at least one defined benefit member and some or all of the contributions it has received paid into a common pool of money and not allocated to an individual member.

A defined benefits superannuation fund can be a public sector superannuation scheme or offered by a private sector employer.

If you are a member of a defined benefits superannuation fund when you retire you will receive either or both of:

— An amount of money based on a formula in the superannuation fund's trust deed

— A benefit based on your salary at a particular date or an average of your salary over a period of time, for example:

Factor x Completed years of service x Final annual salary
= Retirement benefit

Your member's booklet will give you details of how your benefit is worked out.

Let's take an example. Geoff, an employee, retires after 20 years of service on a final annual salary of $50,000. The value of the factor is 0.15 (as determined by the fund's trust deed and trustees). His retirement benefit is $150,000 (0.15 x 20 x $50,000).

If superannuation is in a defined benefit fund it is your employer who bears the investment risk or benefits. This is because it is the employer's level of contributions, based on an actuary's calculations, that ensures that the fund's liabilities can be met.

SUPERANNUATION FUNDS' INVESTMENT STRATEGIES

You may be allowed to choose between different types of accumulation funds or between different types of investment strategies within a single fund. Funds may use labels like growth, balanced, capital stable or capital guaranteed. These classifications of fund's investment options refer to the fund's investment strategy and the fund's expected return.

Before you choose any of these alternatives read the fund's investment strategy carefully and understand the level of return and risk it expects to incur. Be aware that your accumulated superannuation is reduced when the fund makes a loss (a negative return). Below is a summary of the main types of investment options that are offered by large funds from highest to lowest return and risk.

High growth funds

A high growth fund invests all of its money in growth assets such as Australian and international shares, property and alternative investments. This option aims to achieve a return of at least 5 per cent per annum more than inflation over time. Both the risk and return are high to very high and in years where market linked assets fall in value the loss can be severe.

Growth funds

A growth fund generally invests 80 to 85 per cent of its money into growth assets such as Australian and international shares, property and alternative investments, with the balance in fixed interest for higher returns over the long term. This option aims to achieve returns at least 4 per cent above inflation over time. As there can be losses on the growth investments there is a high risk of an overall loss and also the opportunity of high returns when market linked assets increase in value.

Balanced funds

Balanced fund investments provide diversification across shares, property, fixed interest and cash to provide some growth. The amount of return and risk is determined by the proportion of funds invested in each asset. About 60 to 65 per cent is invested in growth assets and the balance in fixed interest and cash. This option aims to achieve a return at least 3 per cent above inflation. As there can be losses on the market linked investments there is a moderate risk of an overall loss occasionally. There is also the opportunity of moderate returns from market linked assets increasing in value.

Conservative balanced funds

Conservative balanced fund investments provide diversification across shares, property, fixed interest and cash to provide some growth. The amount of return and risk is determined by the proportion of funds invested in each area. About half of the investments are in growth assets and half in fixed interest and cash. This option aims to achieve a return at least 2.5 per cent above inflation. As there can be losses on the market linked investments there is a modest risk of an overall loss occasionally. There is also the opportunity of modest returns when market linked assets increase in value.

Capital stable funds

Capital stable fund investments are mainly (about 70 per cent) in fixed interest and cash with the balance in property and Australian and international shares. The aim is to reduce the risk of losing capital. This option aims to achieve returns of at least 2 per cent more than inflation. As there can be losses on the other investments there is still a small risk of an overall loss occasionally.

Cash funds

Cash fund investments are 100 per cent invested in cash and aim to achieve a return at least 1 per cent above inflation.

So which investment option is best? Well, that depends on what will happen in the financial world over the next few years. With the benefit of hindsight if you had been in a high growth fund in 2006-07 and then switched to cash until March 2009 and then switched into a balanced, growth or high growth fund for the remainder of 2009 and into March 2010 you would have achieved the optimum result! If only we could see future trends so well!

Let's look at a case study.

CASE STUDY: High growth versus conservative

Take Kerry, he ticked the 'high growth' box on his investment choice for his superannuation as he thought this option would build up his superannuation benefits more quickly. Kerry is close to retiring and has now found out that his superannuation has had a period of negative growth. What negative growth really means is that the investments made by his superannuation fund have fallen in value and as a result he has lost a substantial amount of his previously accumulated superannuation.

Let's look at what happens when a superannuation account balance goes up and then falls in value over a three year period.

Kerry's superannuation fund had increased in value at 18 per cent for year one and then it fell by 16 per cent in years two and three. He isn't just back to square one, he has less than he started with as is shown by the numbers below:

Opening account balance	$100,000	
Change in year 1 + 18%	$18,000	$118,000
Change in year 2 − 16%	$18,880	$99,120
Change in year 3 − 16%	$15,860	$83,260

The average decrease in the three years is approximately 6 per cent per annum. Kerry will need his fund to grow by 20.1 per cent, just to get it back to his opening balance. It will have to earn 41.7 per cent to get back to the balance his fund was at the end of year one.

What if Kerry had chosen conservative investments and the increase in value was 6 per cent in year one and 5 per cent in year two, followed by a 3 per cent increase in year three?

Opening account balance	$100,000	
Change in year 1 + 6%	$6000	$106,000
Change in year 2 + 5%	$5300	$111,300
Change in year 3 + 3%	$3340	$114,640

This would result in an average increase in the three year period of 4.66 per cent.

The moral of this story is to get rich slowly. All too many retirees find that they have made the wrong investment decision and have not realised it until it is too late. This is especially important when you are close to retirement.

If you think these figures are exaggerated we rounded the annual returns shown in the investment performance of an industry superannuation fund, as reported on its website over the three year period from 2006-07 to 2008-09.

In the table below we show the average returns for each of the above investment options for the three year and five year period before and during the global financial crisis ended in 30 June 2009. We also show the highest and lowest return in any year over a five year period.

Table 7.2 Average, highest and lowest returns of six different investment options

Investment option	Average return 3 year period	Average return 5 year period	Highest return in a year in 5 year period	Lowest return in a year in 5 year period
High growth	-2.5%	5.6%	21.1%	-14.5%
Growth	-2.0%	5.4%	17.5%	-12.7%
Balanced	-0.6%	5.3%	15.1%	-9.1%
Conservative balanced	0.7%	4.9%	11.7%	-5.0%
Capital stable	2.5%	5.0%	9.7%	-0.9%
Cash	4.9%	5.1%	6.1%	3.7%

Now, you are probably thinking that you may as well have had the money in the bank. Well, remember these returns are after taxes and other fees and charges, so depending on your other income you may well have ended up with less in your own hands after paying tax on the earnings.

SELF MANAGED SUPERANNUATION FUNDS

Some people choose to run their self managed superannuation fund (SMSF) to have more control of their superannuation savings.

You may be advised, or make your own decision, to transfer your superannuation benefits into your own SMSF (which is sometimes referred to as a do it yourself or DIY super fund). Transferring money from one superannuation fund to another is called rolling over.

If you are an employee who is eligible to choose the superannuation fund that will receive your employer's contributions you can direct your employer to pay your superannuation entitlement into your SMSF.

If you are thinking of setting up a self managed superannuation fund make sure that you understand what you are doing before you go ahead.

Should you do it yourself?

There are well over 400,000 SMSFs with between one and four members already operating in Australia.

There are a number of trust law and legislative requirements in setting up an SMSF. If you wish to set up your own fund you should consult with a professional adviser before committing to this option.

The first thing you need to do is to have a trust deed prepared, which evidences the existence of the trust and establishes the rules of operation of the fund.

All superannuation funds are required to appoint one or more trustees. Trustees are responsible for ensuring the fund is properly managed and that it complies with superannuation laws, rules and broader legal obligations. In the case of an SMSF all fund members must also be appointed as trustees of the fund or as directors of the trustee company.

The trustees of a superannuation fund must obtain a tax file number (TFN) and Australian Business Number (ABN) for the fund from the Australian Taxation Office (ATO).

The assets of the SMSF must be kept separate from any assets owned personally by any of the trustees or from those belonging to a business (where the owners of a business set up the SMSF).

Trustees are required to draw up and implement an appropriate investment strategy for the investment of the fund's assets.

In addition, trustees need to be aware there are several administrative obligations that must be met throughout the life of the fund. The authors of this book establish, and offer ongoing support for, self managed superannuation funds. Services include preparing all necessary paperwork, applications, and preparing an investment strategy as well as ongoing compliance work. You can obtain more details from their website www.oasiswealth.com.au.

Investment issues with self managed superannuation funds

You can also make personal contributions into your SMSF in cash or in the form of certain assets. You are only allowed to transfer or sell assets that you currently own, or that are owned by a person or entity such as a company or trust that is related to you, if the law allows you to. The assets that you can transfer in this way are quite limited. The main assets that you can transfer from your own name to an SMSF are:

— Securities such as shares that are listed on any approved stock exchange in the world, such as the ASX and the US NASDAQ

— Business real property with no residential use such as a factory, warehouse or shop.

Just because you can transfer these assets doesn't mean that you should do so for one or more of these reasons:

— The value may exceed the limits that the government has placed on the amount of contributions that can be made in a financial year

— Transferring an asset from your own name means that you are treated by tax law as having sold that asset and therefore you may:

- be liable to pay tax on part or all of the capital gain you made, or alternatively

- incur a capital loss that can only be offset against capital gains that you make in that year or a future year, but that cannot be claimed as a tax deduction against your other income.

The upside of transferring the assets that you own personally into the fund is that from that point on, before you commence a superannuation income stream you will only be paying 15 per cent on the fund's taxable income. No tax is paid if your whole fund is paying account based income streams. If the fund receives franked dividends the attached imputation credits will reduce any tax liability the fund has, even tax otherwise payable on concessional contributions. In addition, if you have any excess imputation credits they will be refunded to your fund.

If you own business premises that you use for your business or rent to another business, you can transfer them to the fund as a contribution so long as the value does not exceed your contribution cap. Alternatively you can sell them to the fund. Before doing so get professional advice on the capital gains tax and other implications involved in the transfer. There may also be stamp duty and other costs to pay on transfer in the state or territory where the business real property is located.

If, after considering all factors, it is a viable proposition, the benefit is that you can then rent the business premises to anyone, including yourself or a related party. Of course, if you are renting the premises yourself you must pay rent at the current market value applying to those premises until you retire. When you have retired you can sell the business premises and if you are a small business you can take advantage of one of the tax concessions available or you can rent the business premises to the person you sell the business to, or anyone else who comes along as a tenant for that matter.

The good news is that during the period that you are renting the premises your business can claim a tax deduction for the rent at your current tax rate or, if you operate your business through a company, the company can claim a tax deduction at the company tax rate, but the superannuation fund only pays tax at 15 per cent on the rental income it receives. If you are a sole trader or partner in a partnership you may be able to claim a personal tax deduction for superannuation contributions up to your concessional contributions cap. This can be used to offset part of any capital gain arising from the transfer of the property.

For example if you are a sole trader and you transfer an investment business real property from your own name to your superannuation fund and make a net capital gain of $30,000, you can, if it suits your current circumstances, claim a personal deduction. This deduction can be for a superannuation contribution up to your concessional contributions cap that applies for your age. See the Appendix at the back of this book for the caps applying at the time this book was written.

Once you convert your benefits in the self managed fund into a superannuation income stream the fund will not pay any tax on the income it receives from rent.

CASE STUDY: George and Hannah's superannuation

George and Hannah set up a company recently and have established a land subdivision and development business since then. George and Hannah are both age 45, directors and employees of the company, and have left the profit in the business to increase capital to invest in more land. However, they now want to draw wages.

George was one of those people who didn't believe in superannuation, but his adviser has told him that he has to pay a certain amount of superannuation because of superannuation guarantee rules. These rules require all employers, including companies established and operated by the owners where the owners are also employees, to pay the superannuation guarantee. George islivid; he has some superannuation in a large superannuation fund that has gone backwards. His adviser explained that there were other options that he can consider, including a self managed superannuation fund with a maximum of four members. The fund would need to have sufficient capital (we suggest at least $100,000 or rapidly approaching that amount).

"How can I get more in?" asks George.

"You can salary sacrifice or put in after-tax contributions."

George wasn't clear what that meant so his adviser explained that in simple terms salary sacrifice is where you get your company to pay additional contributions over and above the amount required under the superannuation guarantee requirements, and you take a lower salary. After-tax contributions are superannuation contributions you make yourself from money that has already been taxed. George still didn't much like the idea of superannuation, but being as it had to be paid he and Hannah set up a self managed superannuation fund.

"Now, what can I invest the money in?" asked George. "I only know real estate and that's all I believe in".

He was advised that that would not be a problem so long as his investment strategy allowed it. "What's an investment strategy?" he asked. "It's like a little financial plan for your superannuation fund that outlines what you are going to invest in, what you are aiming to achieve and how you expect to achieve it."

"Not a problem. Now, can we give our fund a property I already own in our own name as an after-tax contribution?"

"Yes, so long as it is within the non-concessional contributions cap and it is business real property, but you can't give the fund a residential property, because the law doesn't allow this."

"Can the fund buy a residential property from someone else?"

"Yes, so long as the owner is not your relative, your employer or a company or trust that you control."

"Why not?"

"No idea, except that the law says you can't and the politicians won't change the law, even though it makes no sense."

George owned two run-down shops in a country town that hadn't increased much in value since he had bought them but had a good rental return. So he put them into the fund and used the contributions from the company to the fund to renovate them. (At that time the shops were valued at $240,000 which was less than George and Hannah's combined non-concessional contributions cap for that year. They were returning $12,000 net rent per year.)

Over the next year after the shops had been renovated they were worth over $400,000, and the return on them was rent of $30,000 per year. Also the tenants paid all of the outgoings such as rates and water rates. The 15 per cent tax the fund paid meant that the after-tax return was about $25,500. George and Hannah plan to put other investments in place in the fund and their adviser has told them that once they retire and convert their accumulated benefits to account based income streams they will pay no tax on the rent and other income.

George is now absolutely hooked on super and tells everyone he meets that they should find out whether a self managed superannuation fund suits them.

RETIREMENT FUNDING WITH SUPERANNUATION

Using superannuation savings as the main source of retirement funding can be a benchmark for retirement income projections. Since the long term projections are based on assumptions, they may be only used as an indication. However, this can provide useful information as to what you need to start doing now to achieve your retirement goals. Retirement funding with superannuation savings can be affected by several factors including:

— Your current superannuation savings
— Your current age and retirement age
— Current rates of interest, inflation and investment returns
— Amount of retirement income required.

When you are commencing a superannuation income stream there are three components in your superannuation – the taxable component and the tax free component, plus the contributions component. These will be used to calculate the taxable component and tax free component of your income stream whilst you are under age 60 and upon your death.

Not everyone has enough superannuation and may decide to purchase an income stream with ordinary money to supplement their income. The retirement reckoner below gives you a guide to the amount of capital you would need to purchase a lifetime income stream. The reason that the income is lower for women than men is because women have a longer life expectancy than men.

Table 7.3 Retirement income stream reckoner

Retirement income stream purchased with ordinary money

Annual income required ($)	Retirement funding estimate	
	Male ($)	Female ($)
30,000	526,316	576,923
40,000	701,754	769,231
50,000	877,193	961,538
60,000	1,052,632	1,153,846
70,000	1,228,070	1,346,154
80,000	1,403,509	1,538,462

Assumptions:
- Net return after tax, fees and charges is 4 per cent per annum
- All contributions to super are based on annual contributions
- Retirement income is based on purchased lifetime income stream payments ($5,700 per annum for every $100,000 for males, $5,200 per annum for every $100,000 for females)
- All income and contributions are in today's dollars.

As we said at the beginning of the chapter, you can review your current superannuation by filling out the checklist in Form 7.1.

Form 7.1 Checklist about your superannuation

- How much is my current balance in superannuation? _____
- How much does my employer contribute annually to superannuation? _____
- How much do I contribute to superannuation? _____
- How much of my contributions are made through salary sacrifice? _____
- How much of my contributions are made out of after-tax money? _____
- What other investments do I have that I can transfer or sell and put into superannuation? _____
- What benefits are currently projected to be from my superannuation at my proposed retirement date? _____

Then you can enter your current contributions and benefit details in Form 7.2.

Form 7.2 Superannuation contributions and benefits details

Superannuation	Type	Self	Partner
Annual contribution	Employer contributions		
Annual contribution	Personal contributions		
Value now			
Current death benefit	Death benefit		
Estimated retirement benefit	All		

CHAPTER 8

Government pensions, payments and support

In this chapter you will learn about:

- The age pension
- The age service pension
- Income and assets tests
- Taxation of pensions
- Limits on giving away assets or income.

Whilst the aim of this book is to help you retire at a time of your own choosing, not that designated by the government, many of you will also qualify for some income or other support from the government when you reach 'retirement age'.

The commonwealth government pays age pensions to eligible senior Australians from the taxes it collects. The problem with relying on government funded regular income is that the terms of eligibility for pension income are then controlled by the government. We all know that the government can and does change the rules at any time it chooses. Successive governments have done so many times in the past to tighten the rules. It is therefore prudent to view government funded pensions as a valuable safety net to top up income from your own sources, particularly if your personally funded retirement income reduces over time, as it did for many retirees during the global financial crisis.

Government funded age pensions provide a regular income for senior Australians, however you are only eligible for a full pension if your income and assets are below the limits prescribed in income and assets tests. These limits for a full pension are indexed on 1 January each year (i.e. they increase in line with inflation) and those limits that apply at the time of writing are included in the Appendix at the back of this book.

The two most common pensions are:

— The age pension paid by Centrelink

— The age service pension paid to veterans by the Department of Veterans' Affairs (DVA).

Both types of pensions are paid fortnightly, based on daily entitlements. The rate of pension that you are entitled to is increased twice yearly, in March and September, in line with movements in the cost of living and/or average wages. The full rates applying at the time of writing are shown in the Appendix at the back of this book.

You cannot receive a service pension from the DVA as well as an age pension or any other social security pension or benefit (the one exception is family tax benefit).

The age that a person can apply for an age pension depends on their gender, date of birth and type of pension. For men, the age pension age is from 65 to 67 and the age service pension age is five years younger at 60 to 62. For women the age pension age is 64 to 67 and age service pension age is five years younger at 59 to 62.

Table 8.1 shows the age when males and females qualify for an age pension. If you qualify for an age service pension then reduce the age shown in Table 8.1 by five years. Please note that all people born before 1946 are already age pension age.

Table 8.1 Qualifying ages for the age pension

Date of birth	Women age pension age	Men age pension age
1 January 1946 to 30 June 1947	64	65
1 July 1947 to 31 December 1948	64½	65
1 January 1949 to 30 June 1952	65	65
1 July 1952 to 31 December 1953	65½	65½
1 January 1954 to 30 June 1955	66	66
1 July 1955 to 31 December 1956	66½	66½
From 1 January 1957	67	67

If you continue working after the pension age that applies to you, and you defer claiming an age or age service pension or the age income support supplement, you may be entitled to the age pension work bonus. This bonus treats employment income concessionally up to a capped amount for income test assessment purposes. If you are still working when you reach age pension age this may apply to you and you should read the section headed 'Age pension work bonus' later in this chapter.

THE AGE PENSION

The age pension may be payable to people who are age pension age. In order to qualify for the age pension, you must be in Australia on the day you lodge your claim and be an Australian resident, (unless you are claiming under an international social security agreement).

You must also satisfy at least one of the following residence requirements:

— You have lived in Australia for at least 10 years, with at least five of these years in one period

— You are a woman who was widowed in Australia while both you and your late partner were Australian residents and you have been a resident for at least two years immediately before making a claim

— You were receiving Widow B pension, Widow Allowance or
Partner Allowance immediately before you reached age
pension age

— You have residence in certain countries with an
international social security agreement with Australia that
counts towards Australian residence

— You have a qualifying residence exemption because you
arrived as a refugee under a special program.

THE AGE SERVICE PENSION

A service pension is payable to eligible veterans, their partners, and
widows and widowers. For service pension purposes, a veteran is a
person who has qualifying service. Eligible veterans include:

— Australian veterans
— Commonwealth veterans
— Allied veterans
— Australian mariners
— Allied mariners.

Age service pension is paid to veterans with qualifying service five
years earlier than the age pension age shown in Table 8.1. This earlier
qualifying age is to recognise that the intangible effects of war may
result in premature ageing and/or loss of earning power (an
invalidity service pension may be granted at any age).

You are eligible for the service pension if you are a veteran who:

— Has qualifying service – generally you have served in
operations against the enemy whilst in danger from hostile
forces of the enemy; and

— Meets the residency requirements – you are a resident of
Australia and are present in Australia at the time of lodging
the claim for service pension (commonwealth veterans and

allied veterans and mariners must generally have been an Australian resident for at least 10 years, although there are some exemptions); and

— Is service pension age; or
— Is permanently blind or is permanently unable to work.

However, even if you are eligible you may still not receive a service pension because of your income and assets which are subject to income and assets tests.

To apply for a service pension you need to contact your nearest DVA office, where an application form will be tailored to suit your circumstances. Application forms are also available from some ex-service organisations, such as the RSL.

PARTNER SERVICE PENSION

A partner service pension may be paid to partners of veterans who are receiving (or are eligible to receive) the service pension. A partner is a person who is legally married to and living with a veteran; legally married to a veteran and separated from that veteran for less than 12 months (unless they are age pension age and have not entered into a de facto relationship); or living in a marriage-like relationship with a veteran.

A partner is eligible for a partner service pension if she or he:

— Is at least 50 years of age; or
— Has dependent children; or
— Is the partner of a veteran who receives the Totally and Permanently Incapacitated (T&PI) disability pension.

The widow or widower of a veteran who was receiving partner service pension immediately before the veteran's death continues to be eligible for that pension. Note that there are other circumstances where a widow or widower of a veteran is eligible for partner service pension and these are contained in the DVA's Fact Sheet IS 45: Partner Service Pension.

RATES OF SERVICE PENSION

There are two different rates of service pension. A singles rate is payable to single pensioners, widows, widowers and partners who are legally married to a veteran but are separated (not divorced). A couples rate is payable to each member of a couple who are living together, whether legally married or living in a marriage-like relationship.

If only one member of a couple receives a service pension, the couples rate of pension is paid. If a couple separates because of ill-health or during a period of respite care, each member of the couple may be paid at the singles rate, however, the couples rate of allowable income and assets value limit applies.

PENSION INCOME AND ASSETS TESTS

The amount of pension you are entitled to receive can be affected by the amount of other income that you receive and/or the value of certain assets that you own. If you are a couple your combined income and the combined value of your assets is used to calculate your pension entitlement.

Your pension will be reduced if your 'assessable income' and/or 'assessable assets' (explained below), as calculated under the income test and the assets test, exceed the allowable limits that entitle you to the maximum rate of pension.

The amount of pension that you may be entitled to under the assets test is compared to the amount that can be paid under the income test. The pension you are entitled to is the lower of these two amounts.

If your allowable income and allowable assets (combined if you are a couple) remain within the applicable threshold you will be entitled to the maximum rate of pension.

Note that there is no income and assets test for legally blind pensioners.

Income

The amount of income you or your partner receives can affect the amount of pension you are entitled to. The way income is assessed depends on where this income comes from.

Your income is any money, valuable consideration or profits you may have earned, derived or received and deemed income on certain investments. However payments from Centrelink or the DVA are excluded from the income test.

Amounts that are included in assessable income which is used to calculate eligibility for age pension under the income test are:

— Deemed income from financial investments, e.g. term deposits, shares, bank accounts, including overseas investments and, if you have reached pension age, superannuation or rollover funds (see 'Deemed income' below)

— Income paid from income streams

— Gross (before tax) income from earnings, including certain fringe benefits, less the work bonus (see below)

— Voluntary concessional (before tax) personal superannuation contributions and employment income salary sacrificed into superannuation (see 'reportable superannuation contributions' below)

— Net income from self-employment and businesses, including family businesses and farms

— Net income from rental property, including rental holiday homes

— Total net losses from rental property

— Total net investment losses from financial investments

— Income from deceased estates

— Compensation payments

— Income from boarders or lodgers

— Distributions that you receive or which are distributed to you in the accounts of a family trust

— Dividends from private company shares

— Income from overseas pensions.

Reportable superannuation contributions

Reportable superannuation contributions include discretionary concessional (before tax) superannuation contributions. They must be included when you estimate your income to Centrelink. Reportable superannuation contributions are:

— Voluntary salary sacrificed superannuation contributions made by you or on your behalf by your employer. These voluntary contributions are over and above those required under superannuation guarantee rules, that is over 9 per cent of income or under an industrial award

— Total superannuation contributions made by you that you claim as a tax deduction as a self-employed person or investor.

Personal non-concessional (after-tax) contributions are excluded from reportable superannuation contributions and do not have to be reported.

Example: Reportable superannuation contributions. Ava, age 63, salary sacrifices 5 per cent of her salary into superannuation. This contribution is above the 9 per cent superannuation guarantee contribution that her employer already makes. Ava's annual salary is $20,000. It is compulsory for her employer to contribute 9 per cent, or $1,800. This compulsory amount is not a reportable superannuation contribution and so does not need to be reported. Ava's contribution of 5 per cent ($1,000) is a reportable superannuation contribution and must be declared. Ava's taxable income is $19,000, but the assessable income that must be declared for the income test relating to income support payments is based on an annual income of $20,000 whilst she is under age pension age, and reported fortnightly.

Total net losses from rental property and financial investment income

In addition to net rental property losses, total net investment losses are included as assessable income. The amount included is the sum of net losses from rental property income plus net losses from financial investment income. When net losses from rental property income and net losses from financial investment income are added together they are referred to as total net investment losses.

If you expect to make a loss from rental property income, financial investment income, or both, you need to give details of the total amount of losses to Centrelink.

It is important that you understand that you only need to record losses from investment earnings. Investment earnings include taxable and tax-exempt interest, dividends and rental income. Capital losses (the difference between the purchase price and sale price, where an asset is sold for less than it was purchased for) are not added back for income test purposes.

Example: Loss from financial investment income. David buys shares at a cost of $12,000. He borrows $10,000 from the bank at 8 per cent interest to buy them. The shares pay annual unfranked dividends of 5 per cent, or $600, but the interest on his loan is $800. This means David makes a net investment loss of $200 ($800 interest − $600 dividends). David's gross income is $50,000. After this loss, his taxable income would be $49,800 ($50,000 − $200). However, the income he must declare for income test purposes is $50,000.

Example: Loss from rental property income and financial investment income. Elle calculates that she will make a loss of $5,000 from rental property income and a loss from financial investment income of $2,000. The Tax Office assesses Elle's taxable income as $23,000. Her total net investment losses are $7,000 ($5,000 + $2,000) and she must add these back to her taxable income, making her assessable income $30,000 for income test purposes.

Deemed income

You do not have to provide details of income received from your financial investments because Centrelink or the DVA will assume or 'deem' that your financial investments are earning a certain amount of income, regardless of the income they actually earn. (See the Appendix at the back of this book for the deeming rates applicable to your circumstances at the time of writing.)

This means that if the actual income you receive from your investments exceeds your deemed income, that extra is ignored when your rate of pension is worked out. Financial investments are:

— Bank, building society and credit union accounts
— Term deposits and debentures
— Friendly society bonds
— Managed investments
— Listed shares and securities
— Shares in unlisted public companies
— Gold and other bullion
— Certain income streams
— Approved deposit funds, deferred annuities and superannuation fund investments held by people over age pension age
— Short-term assets tested income streams
— Loans, including those to family trusts and companies

— The amount of money or other assets you give away of more than $10,000 in a financial year (and $30,000 in five years) (see 'Limits on giving away assets or income' below).

Allowable income

Allowable income is the amount of income assessed before the pension reduces, and depends on whether you are single or a couple.

These limits are indexed on 1 July each year, and the current limits are listed in the Appendix at the back of this book.

If you have dependent children, the allowable income increases by $24.60 per fortnight for each dependent child.

Income above the allowable income, or assets value limit, reduces the amount of pension payable by 50¢ for each additional dollar of income you receive each year if you are single and by 25¢ each if you are a couple. For example, if you are single and your income exceeds the allowable income by $100 per fortnight your fortnightly pension will be reduced by $50 per fortnight. If you are a couple and you are both receiving a pension, each of your pensions will be reduced by $25 per fortnight.

Where a pensioner has a partner who is not yet entitled to a pension and so is receiving an allowance such as partner allowance, the combined income of both partners is used to assess the rate of payment for each member of a couple. This is done using the couples pension income test for the pensioner and the allowee income test on half of the income for the allowee.

Example: Pensioner with a non-pensioner partner. Jimmy is an age pensioner and his partner Marjorie is receiving the Newstart Allowance. The pension free area for couples is deducted from the joint income then Jimmy's pension is reduced by 25¢ in the dollar for any amount over the allowable income.

Marjorie's rate of partner allowance will depend on the more punitive allowance income test. Half of the joint total income is used to calculate the amount that may affect her partner allowance. If this amount does not exceed $62 her allowance will not be reduced. If it is between $62 and $250 per fortnight her partner allowance will reduce by 50¢ in the dollar for every dollar of income between $62 and $250. If it exceeds $250, her partner allowance will reduce by $94 plus 60¢ in the dollar for every dollar of income in excess of $250.

Work bonus

The government rewards ongoing workforce participation for people who have reached pension age by way of a work bonus. The work bonus treats earned income up to a capped amount concessionally and the concessional amount is in addition to the normal allowable income threshold.

Under the work bonus only half of the capped amount of earned income in each instalment period (a maximum of 14 days) is counted in the income test for people over pension age. The capped amount is increased by CPI on 1 July each year. Income over the capped amount is all included in the income test. The capped amount until 30 June 2010 is $500, then it is increased by CPI annually from 1 July 2010.

Example: Work bonus cap. John is a single person over age pension age. His only income is earnings of $600 a fortnight. If the capped rate is $500 he will have $350 assessed as income, calculated:

$600 earnings – $500 cap	$100
$500 cap x 50 per cent	$250
Assessed income	$350

TAXATION OF PENSIONS

Most pensions are assessable income for taxation purposes and are therefore taxable. If you receive a taxable pension Centrelink or the DVA will issue you with a Payment Summary at the end of each financial year showing the amount of pension you have received.

Generally, your pension plus income below the allowable income is the only income you have received, so you will not have to lodge a tax return for that year.

Assessable assets

Assets are any property or item of value that you or your partner own or have an interest in, both inside and outside Australia.

Your assessable assets are those that are counted to work out your age or age service pension entitlement. They include:

— The total amount you have in bank, building society or credit union accounts, term deposits, bonds, debentures and shares

— The value of your investments in property trusts, friendly societies, equity trusts, mortgage trusts and bond trusts

— If you are age pension age, the total amount you have invested in approved deposit funds, deferred annuities and superannuation funds

— Income streams, such as account based, or allocated pensions and allocated annuities, that do not satisfy assets test exemption rules

— Real estate including vacant land and holiday homes, and, if you operate a business at home, any part of your home that is used primarily or solely for business purposes

— Property other than your principal home and up to two hectares of attached land

— The net value of farms and businesses including goodwill, buildings and machinery

— Loans, including interest free loans to private companies/ businesses, family trusts, etc.

— Motor vehicles

— Boats and caravans unless used as your principal home

— Household contents including furniture, antiques, paintings and other works of art, soft furnishings and electrical appliances (but not fixtures in your home such as stoves and built-in items)

— Your personal effects, including jewellery

— Investment collections of coins, stamps and so on

— The amount of money or other assets that you give away that exceed $10,000 in a financial year (and $30,000 in five years). (See 'Limits on giving away assets or income' below.)

Exempt or disregarded assets

Some assets, called exempt assets, are excluded from the assets test. These include:

— The home you live in, and up to two hectares of land around your home that you use for domestic purposes

— Income streams (pensions and annuities) that have all of the required characteristics to be classified as assets test exempt

— All superannuation/rollover investments until you reach age pension age

— Any property or monies left to you in an estate which you have not yet received

— A funeral bond that currently does not exceed $10,750 and is indexed in line with CPI

— An advance payment for a cemetery plot and funeral services

— Aids for people with a disability

— Vehicles provided by the DVA under the Vehicle Assistance Scheme (gift car scheme)

— Proceeds from the sale of your principal home which you intend to use, within 12 months, to purchase another home

— Most compensation or insurance payments for loss or damage to buildings or personal effects.

The 'value' of your assets

You will need to provide Centrelink or the DVA with your own estimate of the net market value of your assessable assets. This estimate is the amount of money you would get if you sold the asset now, less any debts on the asset such as registered mortgages, hire purchase debts or loans.

Example: Value of assets. You paid $20,000 for a boat and still owe $8,000 on it. You could get $13,000 if you sold it, so that is its market value. Its net market value is $5,000 ($13,000 from the sale less $8,000 that you still owe). Therefore the amount counted as an assessable asset is $5,000.

Centrelink or the DVA may get the Valuer General's Office to value real estate that you own. If you are not happy with the valuation that is placed on a piece of real estate that you own, ask for it to be reassessed. We know of one retiree couple whose holiday home was re-valued and as a result their pension was cut to virtually nothing. They were shocked and asked for the valuation to be reviewed and the valuation was cut by $80,000. As a result their combined pension increased by $1.50 for each $1,000 reduction in the valuation, and so their combined pension increased by $120 per fortnight.

Allowable asset limit

The pension assets test reduces your pension rate if the value of your assets exceeds the allowable asset limit and up to the asset cut-off limit. There are four allowable asset limits which depend on whether you are single or a couple and whether you are a homeowner or a non-homeowner. The categories are:

— Single homeowners

— Single non-homeowners

— Couples who are homeowners

— Couples who are non-homeowners.

Assets above the allowable asset limit reduce the amount of pension payable by $1.50 per fortnight for each additional $1,000 of assets you have and your pension cuts out when your assets exceed the cut-off limit. For example, if your assets exceed the assets value limit by $20,000 your fortnightly pension will be reduced by $30 if the assets test is the means test that results in you receiving the least pension. These limits are indexed on 1 July each year, and those that applied at the time of writing are listed in the Appendix at the back of this book.

If you are a couple you will be treated as if you receive half of your combined income and you each own half your combined assets, regardless of who actually receives the income or owns the assets. This means that you will both be paid the same rate of pension.

Assessment of income streams

Centrelink or the DVA look at different types of income streams (pensions and annuities) in different ways. They have divided them into three main categories when they assess how much age or service age pension you are entitled to. These categories of income streams are provided in the following table.

Table 8.2 Income streams

Category	Income stream types included in this category	Income and assets tests
1. **Short Term Assets Tested** (fixed term of 5 years or less)	Most non account based income streams which are for a fixed term of 5 years or less	Income test: Deeming rules apply Asset test: Asset test applies
2. **Long Term Assets Tested** (a fixed term in excess of 5 years, and all other income streams that do not meet the specific requirements of Category 3)	• all account based (allocated) income streams • fixed term income streams with terms of more than 5 years • lifetime income streams that are not complying.	Income test: Income is reduced by an amount of exempt income Asset test: Asset test applies
3. **Long Term Assets Test Exempt** (all non-account based lifetime and certain fixed term income streams)*	• Lifetime income streams with all required characteristics • Fixed term income streams payable for life expectancy with all the required characteristics • Account based market linked income streams which have all the required characteristics	Income test: Income is reduced by an amount of exempt income Asset test: 50 per cent assets test exemption if it is commenced before 20 September 2007. A 100 per cent assets test exemption applies for complying income streams commenced before 20 September 2004.

* Since 20 September 2007, all income streams are fully assets tested.

Superannuation benefits in your superannuation fund are taken into account once you reach age or service pension age.

Extra allowable amount for retirement village and granny flat residents

If your entry contribution to your retirement village and granny flat is equal to or less than the difference between the non-homeowner and homeowner asset test limits (see Appendix at the back of this book) you will be assessed as a non-homeowner and you may be entitled to rent assistance. Your entry contribution is counted as an asset.

LIMITS ON GIVING AWAY ASSETS OR INCOME

It is important to be aware of the rules that apply to giving your assets or income away within five years of age pension age or you may get a nasty shock when you apply for a pension.

There are restrictions on the amount of assets that you can give away, and where your gifts exceed the allowable limits, your pension may be affected. The limits that apply before your pension may be affected are up to the lesser of:

— $10,000 in a financial year; or

— $30,000 in a rolling 5-year period.

Both limits apply to single people and couples. Any amount that you give away over either of these limits is assessed as a deprived asset and counted as an asset under the assets test for five years from the date of the gift. It is also deemed to be earning income at the prevailing deeming rate under the income test, for five years from when it was given away. These rules also apply to assets that you give away during the five year period before your pension is granted.

In most cases it is better to retain your assets rather than gifting just to increase your age pension!

Example: Gifting assets. Fred and Margaret own a rental property with a net market value of $300,000 which they sell to their son for $160,000. Effectively they have given their son a gift of $140,000, the difference in the value of the property and the amount they received. They therefore have a deprived asset of $130,000 ($140,000 gift less the gifting free area of $10,000) that will be counted as an asset and a financial investment for five years from the date of the gift.

If you transfer your shares or units in a fixed trust or private company, and do not receive full market value for the transferred assets, you will also be considered to have made a gift.

If you relinquish control of a private trust or company after 1 January 2002, you will be considered to have gifted all the assets held by the trust or company.

These gifting rules do not apply to assets that you use to meet your personal expenses such as ongoing living expenses, medical expenses, a holiday, home improvements or car expenses.

If you decide not to receive income that you are entitled to receive, such as a foreign pension, that income will still count as if you were actually receiving it indefinitely.

Example: Not receiving income. George is entitled to receive a foreign pension of $2,000 per year, but decides to forgo it because his age pension would be reduced. George will be assessed by Centrelink as if he were receiving the $2,000 per year indefinitely.

Importantly, regardless of the amount you can give away, think carefully about the effect it may have on your current and future finances. Is it really sensible to be giving your assets away in order to get a small amount of additional pension?

Too many assets and not enough income

If you have assets but little or no income you are expected to rearrange your affairs to provide income for yourself. Where this is not possible you will be taken to be in severe financial hardship if:

— Your total income (including any pension paid under the assets test) is less than the maximum pension rate
— You do not have readily available funds of more than $6,000 if you are single or $10,000 combined if you are a couple
— There is no other course of action that you could be expected to take to improve your financial position.

Hardship provisions

The hardship provisions apply if:

— Your pension is reduced or not payable because of the assets test

— You own an asset which you cannot sell or be reasonably expected to sell

— You cannot borrow against the asset

— Deprivation provisions do not apply

— You are in severe financial hardship because of the assets test

— You would qualify for a pension under the income test.

The rate of payment depends on each individual case and is calculated using a special formula.

Pension loans scheme

The other alternative is to receive income using the Pension Loans Scheme. This is a loan against your assets that provides you with a fortnightly pension for a period ranging from a short time to an indefinite period.

You need to be pension age and only able to get a part pension, or unable to get a pension because of either your income or your assets (but not both). You can decide on the amount you will receive, up to the maximum pension rate, pension supplement and rent assistance each fortnight reduced by any pension you are entitled to receive. The amounts you receive are treated as a loan and are not taxable.

However, compound interest is charged on the balance of the loan that accumulates and is added to the amount of the loan to be repaid. Any real estate that you own in Australia, including your home, may be used as security for the debt. A charge is registered with the Land Titles Office on the title deed of the property you offer as security and you have to pay for any costs relating to this charge. If you own more than one piece of real estate you can exclude one from being offered as security.

If you are affected by the assets test it is better to use the real estate that is assessed as an asset rather than your own home. This is because as the loan increases the value of your assets will decrease and so your pension entitlement will increase over time.

Example: Assets used as security. Ted and Jenny have real estate worth $400,000, their own home is valued at $220,000 and a holiday home is valued at $180,000. It may be better to use the holiday home as security as $180,000 is currently assessed as an asset.

You can repay the loan at any time or it can be repaid from your estate after you die. If on the death of a member of a couple the survivor is using the encumbered asset, the debt will only need to be repaid after the survivor dies.

If you wish to sell the real estate that you are using as security for this loan, you should contact Centrelink or the DVA before arranging the sale so the loan is repaid at the time of the sale.

Pension supplement

The pension supplement is paid fortnightly to help people who receive an age pension (and certain other income support) to meet the costs of daily household and living expenses.

Rent assistance

Rent assistance is payable to pensioners who pay private rent for their accommodation, subject to minimum rent limits.

Remote area allowance

This is payable to pensioners and allowees who live in designated remote areas of Australia, however the income zone tax offset is reduced by the amount of the allowance paid.

Pensioner concession card

If you are granted a pension you will receive a pensioner concession card. This card will entitle you to various commonwealth, state and local government benefits and concessions. These concessions are set by the authorities providing them and so will vary, depending on where you live.

The DVA issues one of the following two health cards to eligible veterans and war widows and widowers, providing health care at the expense of the Department:

— The Gold Card – treatment and health services for all conditions

— The White Card – treatment and health services for specific conditions only.

COMMONWEALTH SENIORS HEALTH CARD (CSHC)

People of age pension age who are not eligible for a full or part age pension may be eligible for an adjusted taxable income tested Commonwealth Seniors Health Card (CSHC). Adjusted taxable income includes:

— Taxable income

— Foreign income that is not subject to income tax in Australia

— Employer provided benefits such as cars, mortgage repayments and health insurance. The amount in excess of $1,000 forms part of a person's adjusted taxable income

— Reportable superannuation contributions

— Total net investment losses.

The total of these items determines whether the adjusted taxable income is below the relevant CSHC income test limit.

The benefits you will receive if you do qualify for a CSHC include:

— A discount on prescription medicines through the Pharmaceutical Benefits Scheme (PBS)

— Bulk-billed general practitioner appointments (at the discretion of the GP)

— A reduction in the cost of out-of-hospital medical expenses above a concessional threshold, through Medicare safety net

— Discounts on Great Southern Rail services such as The Indian Pacific, The Ghan and The Overland

— Additional health, household, transport, education and recreation concessions which may be offered by state or territory and local governments and private providers, the availability of these concessions can vary from state to state.

Once you reach age pension age and your adjusted taxable income is below the capped amount of $50,000 if you are single, $80,000 combined if you are a couple, and $100,000 combined if you are a couple separated by illness (these amounts are increased by $639.60 for each dependent child you care for) you can claim your CSHC by lodging a Commonwealth Seniors Health Card claim form. Couples can lodge their claims on one claim form. You must also provide:

— A minimum of 50 points of identity and proof of Australian Residence

— Proof of your income.

If you are entitled to a CSHC you may also be entitled to receive the Seniors Supplement Allowance which is a non-taxable payment made every three months to help with ongoing bills such as energy, rates and motor vehicle registration fees.

Our overall suggestion is that if feasible the government's pensions and benefits should be viewed as a last resort for your retirement income needs. Our objective in this book is to help you so that you will be self-sufficient for life.

CHAPTER 9

A good early retirement plan

In this chapter you will learn to:

- Save as much as you can
- Build a cash reserve for emergencies
- Review and where necessary rearrange finances
- Reduce financial risk.

SAVE AS MUCH AS YOU CAN FROM TODAY

You must start your early retirement saving and debt reduction plan from today. Sit down and write a list of your non-essential expenditure by reviewing the budget information you prepared in chapter 3. (If you haven't got round to preparing your budget do it now!) Only you can identify your non-essential expenditure and the ways you can reduce it, but here are a few suggestions to get you started:

— Cut your costs when you are outside your home. Save money by preparing your own lunch instead of buying takeaway. Drinks are often highly priced when you are out so you can save a substantial amount of money if you reduce the number of cups of coffee or tea, and glasses of beer or wine you buy when eating out, and replace soft drink and bottled water with tap water.

— Cut your costs at home. Find ways to go 'green' and save on your energy bills. Replace your old light globes with low energy globes (check whether your supplier will do this as a free service). Go solar when your hot water service needs replacing and in the meantime turn the thermostat down a few degrees. Get into the habit of turning off lights whenever you leave a room and turning off your electrical goods at the power point when they are not in use. Try replacing the herbal tea bags you buy with fresh mint or other herbs from your garden or window box – it will save you a lot of money.

— Save money by driving less. Don't take the car if you can walk. Plan your shopping trip so that you buy what you need at the one time. If there are two of you and it is practical for your family circumstances have one family car instead of two and one of you use public transport if you both need to travel.

— If you are a smoker stop smoking today. You are paying extra taxes to the government every time you buy a packet of cigarettes and you will be able to retire earlier than if you continue.

— Cut the cost of your leisure activities and holidays. Look for cut price specials and last minute deals, stay in cheaper hotels.

HAVE A CASH RESERVE FOR EMERGENCIES

Unexpected expenses can arise at any time for property repairs, medical expenses and so on. Unexpected loss of income can also occur from loss of a job or a failed investment. It is good practice to set aside a cash reserve so while you are saving and building your assets for retirement you do not have to disturb your retirement savings when an emergency does arise. We suggest you aim to have at least three months' salary or business income in reserve. If you don't have this much available now, start to build it up today from the savings you have made by cutting your expenditure. If you have a mortgage that allows you to pay off additional amounts and it has a redraw facility increase your regular repayments so that you build up your cash reserve within your mortgage. This will give you a readily available emergency fund should you ever need it. You will also be reducing the outstanding loan, reducing the interest you pay and as a result shortening the term of the loan considerably.

Once you are no longer earning a regular income you need some cash in reserve to pay for unexpected expenses. It is up to you to decide how much you need based on the amount, liquidity and type of your other assets. As a suggestion, you may keep about $10,000 in an interest bearing cash management account that you can access immediately and a further $20,000 in a rolling short-term deposit that can be accessed fairly easily should the need arise.

REVIEW AND REARRANGE INVESTMENTS

It is important to review the investments you own, including superannuation, both as you are building assets and as you approach retirement. This allows you to assess whether you want to continue to hold them or whether some other investments would be more suitable. You should review what each asset is costing you and its potential to grow in value. If it does not have much potential you should consider selling it and placing the money in an income earning investment or in superannuation because when you retire you are going to need regular income.

If you have any debt you should review how you can reduce or even eliminate it.

If you are one of the many Australians who receive some age pension when you reach your age pension age, make sure that your mortgage is secured by your income earning property, not your own home, otherwise it will not reduce your assets for asset test purposes.

If you have assets that will affect your entitlement to a full or part age pension, but those assets do not provide sufficient income to meet your needs, you should consider whether you should rearrange your affairs to improve your income. This may involve the possible disposal of a piece of real estate that is not providing sufficient income or that is using up other income to retain it. For example, you may own vacant land. Vacant land costs you money each year because you need to pay rates and other outgoings, which may include water rates, land tax and grass or weed control. That may be fine whilst you are working but will drain your income when you retire. If you plan to apply for a commonwealth government pension vacant land will be counted as an asset and so may reduce the amount of pension you can receive under the assets test. If the land is increasing rapidly in value then you may wish to keep it, but remember the value needs to increase by the amount of income you are forgoing on the value of the land plus the costs of holding that land. Otherwise you may as well sell it and find a better investment.

Let's say that you own a block of land that cost you $100,000 including stamp duty and other purchase costs three years ago. It has increased in value at 10 per cent of the original cost each year so that it is now valued at $130,000. You are feeling pretty good about that, but look at the facts. If you sell it the selling costs will be about $5,000. You have also paid rates and other costs of owning the land of $5,300 over the three years and interest of 6.5 per cent on an interest-only loan of $60,000, a total of $11,700 over the three years. That block of land has cost you $22,000 to hold over the three year period. You haven't made a 10 per cent gain on the original cost, you have made a gain of 2.66 per cent of the original cost each year. However, as you borrowed this is not a fair measure, because you only outlaid $40,000, so in fact your gain has been 6.66 per cent each year.

Has this been a good investment and will it continue to increase in value at the same rate? That is for you to decide. Whether it is a suitable investment when you are retired is a different matter, and that is the issue you now need to look at.

Will you be able to continue to pay the interest on the loan plus rates and other costs, which will be about $6,000 each year or $115 per week? If not, you need to think about your alternatives. These are to:

— Use other capital that you have to build on the land so that you can generate rent

— Sell the land and invest the after-tax proceeds of about $46,800 ($40,000 + the capital gain of $8,000 reduced by tax payable on 50 per cent of the gain).

Even the most simple of investments such as a short term fixed interest investment of 5 per cent per annum will give you income of $2,340 per year. However it will not give you any capital growth.

PRESERVE AND PROTECT YOUR ASSETS

You need to take measures to preserve and protect the assets you build for your retirement. There are several things to be aware of.

Diversification

Never put all of your eggs in one basket; if something goes wrong with the investment you can lose most or all of your investment, or have the income from your investment frozen and devastate your retirement plans. There are many examples of where this has happened to investors who adopted this approach. Limited diversification into 10 to 12 different quality investments across asset classes and within asset classes will limit your loss to less than 10 per cent of your total assets if you do make a poor investment decision, even if one of the investments turns out to be worthless for whatever reason.

Partly paid shares or units

Don't invest into partly paid shares or units unless you have sufficient capital available to pay the call when it is made. In 2008 investors bought substantial quantities of partly paid stapled units in a toll road for one-tenth of a cent only to find that they were liable to pay a call of $1 per unit, which many could not afford to pay.

Insurance

Insurance is an important part of wealth protection. You should focus on high value assets such as buildings, your life and your income. Insure assets that can result in a high claim against you such as your car and insure your business if there is a possibility you can be sued.

Never be a guarantor

Never provide a guarantee for anyone else's loan, overdraft or rent and this includes for your children or your partner. Why anyone would even consider signing as a guarantor for a loan that they get no benefit from is beyond our comprehension. If a financial institution wants a guarantor for a loan, it means that the person they are lending to is high risk, and you are agreeing to be responsible for the debt or obligation of the other person at the risk of your own assets. If the borrower defaults on the loan you will be liable for the amount outstanding plus interest and default interest and other costs. It is like giving someone a book of signed blank cheques without a time limit and can result in you losing your own assets. If you really must help the person involved lend them the money yourself, at least the amount you lend is the limit you will lose.

We are familiar with a case where a mother had worked hard for 40 years to buy six investment properties and some blue chip shares. When she retired she was able to live comfortably on the rental income and dividends. A few years ago she was asked to sign a guarantee for her son's business loan. The business became unprofitable during the global financial crisis and the loan was increased because he was unable to pay the interest or loan repayments. Her signature on a piece of paper as a guarantor for that loan has resulted in the mother being forced to sell her investment properties, which are her main source of income.

Directors of companies should try to avoid signing guarantees for a company loan or rent because unless they ensure that their personal guarantee ends at the same time as their association with the company they may find themselves liable years after they have left the company. If you have already signed a guarantee discuss it with the person you have signed for and try to get a release from the lender or landlord as fast as you can.

Capital protection products and ongoing payments

Some fund managers offer managed investment products with a capital protection to a fixed date often five to seven years in the future. They are often funded with a 100 per cent investment loan and income flowing from the investment is used to pay the interest on the loan. Initially they appear to be a good and safe investment, but there are issues you need to be aware of.

You need to pay the interest on the loan by 30 June each year, regardless of the amount of income the investment has generated. In a falling market where the fund is making a loss all of the capital can be placed in cash deposits and no further distributions occur. In addition, if the fund 'makes' a distribution it can retain and then compulsorily reinvest that distribution back into the fund to maintain the fund's capital, (even though the distribution is taxable to the investor), and the investor still has to pay the interest on the loan.

The capital protection only exists at the end of the term so if the investor tries to get out of the investment the investment is valued at that time and an early swap break fee and early repayment fees are incurred. This can result in the investor having a bill of several thousands of dollars to pay. If the investor remains in the fund to the end and the fund continues to keep the distributions it appears that the investor will only get part of his or her capital back to pay off the loan as part of it comprises distributions that the investor has not received. If protection of capital is important please take these factors into account and consider alternatives such as term deposits.

MINIMISE RISK WHILST KEEPING SOME ASSETS THAT GROW IN VALUE

It is important for you to design a good early retirement plan that has a balanced approach to maximising your income, and minimising your investment risks. You need to have diversified assets that contain some assets that can grow in value whilst providing income and some that provide higher income so that you can live comfortably and receive at least some age or age service pension where this is possible and appropriate.

We explained how the commonwealth government means tests apply to age pension in chapter 8.

CHAPTER 10

Strategies for early retirement income

In this chapter you will learn about:
- A tax deduction strategy for superannuation
- A co-contribution strategy
- A spouse contribution strategy
- Transition to retirement income streams
- Creating tax free income for retirement.

E ach year consider what you can do to be able to retire early. Make decisions that will build your assets rather than squandering money that could have been invested on useless consumer goods. Take advantage of tax breaks, tax offsets and other benefits year by year as your circumstances or legislation changes, including rules on superannuation. If you have a life partner, working as a team with a common goal of building your retirement savings, will have a multiplier effect. It will increase your chances of retiring early. We realise that this will not be acceptable to some couples, especially those with children from previous relationships, who prefer to keep their assets separate. Remember, though, if you do work on your retirement planning together and your relationship breaks down, you will probably be required to split the assets built up during your relationship equally anyway.

In our opinion superannuation offers the best opportunities to build your wealth year on year. There are many strategies you can employ to take advantage of the various government tax breaks and benefits that superannuation offers. They will not all suit your circumstances but it is still good to explore them.

TAX DEDUCTION STRATEGY FOR SUPERANNUATION

Getting a deduction for concessional contributions can save tax and is particularly effective in a year when you realise a capital gain. If you are an employee and your employer allows you to salary sacrifice into superannuation take advantage of the opportunity to reduce your assessable income.

If you are self-employed or an investor contribute as much as you can afford to without exceeding your contributions caps. Then claim a deduction to reduce your tax on other income.

The strategy shown in the following example assumes that David's transitional concessional contributions cap is $50,000 and Joanne's concessional contributions cap is $25,000.

Example: Tax deduction for superannuation. David age 50 and Joanne age 46 run a business as a partnership and share the profit equally. They haven't contributed anything to superannuation in the last two years, but the business has picked up now and they estimate the taxable profit of the business will be about $150,000. They have just sold an investment property that they owned in joint names for $425,000 and have made a taxable capital gain of $60,000. They want to put the proceeds from the sale into superannuation and reduce the tax on the capital gain and their other income. It will all help towards their goal of an early retirement.

	David	Joanne	Joint
Share of taxable business profit	$75,000	$75,000	$150,000
Share of capital gain	$30,000	$30,000	$60,000
Taxable income without superannuation deduction	**$105,000**	**$105,000**	**$210,000**
Less deduction for superannuation	$50,000	$25,000	$75,000
Taxable income after superannuation deduction	**$55,000**	**$80,000**	**$135,000**
Estimated personal tax saved	$17,350	$9,500	$26,850

They still have $350,000 which they can contribute as a non-concessional contribution. There are many alternatives available, depending on their willingness to work on their early retirement plan in the most tax effective way. If the whole amount is contributed to David's account they can access it four years earlier as a tax effective superannuation income stream or lump sum. Alternatively if they want to keep their superannuation more equal and not trigger the non-concessional contribution cap bring forward rule for both, David could receive $150,000 into his account and Joanne $200,000 into her account.

CO-CONTRIBUTION STRATEGY

People under age 71 at the end of the financial year are eligible for a superannuation co-contribution if all of the following apply:

— They make personal superannuation contributions by 30 June in a financial year into a complying superannuation fund or RSA and do not claim all of it as a tax deduction

— Their total income (less any business deductions) is lower than the maximum income threshold

— 10 per cent or more of their total income is from eligible employment, carrying on a business or a combination of both

— They do not hold an eligible temporary resident visa at any time during the year, unless they are a New Zealand resident or holder of a prescribed visa

— They lodge an income tax return for the relevant financial year.

For 2010 and later financial years the income threshold is your total income (less business deductions) which is the sum of your assessable income, your reportable fringe benefits and your reportable superannuation contributions.

From 1 July 2009 until 30 June 2012 for every dollar of after-tax money you contribute, you can receive up to a dollar co-contribution from the government up to a maximum co-contribution of $1,000 a year. However, this amount is reduced by 3.333¢ for every dollar your total income is over the minimum income threshold amount and the maximum income threshold amount is the minimum income threshold plus $30,000 (the thresholds that apply at the time of writing are shown in the Appendix at the back of this book).

Superannuation guarantee contributions paid by your employer and salary sacrifice contributions, personal contributions that you have claimed an income tax deduction on and contributions made by your spouse or any other party on your behalf, do not qualify for a co-contribution.

If eligible for a co-contribution, you will receive the lesser amount calculated from the following:

— $1,000 − [(total income* − $minimum income threshold) x 0.03333]

— Your total eligible personal superannuation contributions up to a maximum of $1,000

*Total income is the sum of assessable income, reportable fringe benefits and reportable superannuation contributions.

Example: Co-contribution. Rebecca had total income of $37,920 and made after-tax superannuation contributions of $900 by 30 June 2010. Her co-contribution is calculated:

$1,000 − [($37,920 − $31,920) x 0.03333] = $800

Her total eligible personal superannuation contribution is $900.

Rebecca will receive a co-contribution of the lesser of the two amounts, which is $800.

SPOUSE CONTRIBUTION STRATEGY

If you can, make additional contributions into superannuation before converting the account to an income stream. If you are not eligible to contribute to your own account because you are over age 65 and not working you may be able to make contributions for your spouse if he or she is under age 65. The limits on how much you can contribute for your spouse are shown in the Appendix. If you have taxable income and a tax liability you can claim an 18 per cent tax offset on up to the first $3,000 (that is up to $540) on the spouse contribution if your spouse has total income (assessable income plus reportable fringe benefits and reportable superannuation contributions) of $10,800 or less. A partial claim may be payable if the total income is over $10,800 and under $13,800. Accumulating superannuation is not means tested for age pension purposes for you whilst your spouse is under age pension age.

A spouse contribution strategy can provide advantages when the spouse's superannuation is converted into an income stream because:

— Earnings on the assets underlying the income stream are tax free

— Spouse contributions are all treated as a tax free component

— Earnings form part of the taxable component and your spouse can claim a 15 per cent tax offset on the taxable component on amounts received whilst he or she is age 55 to under 60

— Once your spouse reaches age 60 all of the income from the income stream is tax free

— If you or your spouse's age pension is reduced due to the income test by a superannuation income stream it can result in more age pension due to the favourable rules applied to superannuation income streams.

Example: Spouse contribution strategy. Alexander is age 66 and retired last May and his spouse Emma is age 60 and has not worked since their children were born. She has no superannuation and has a cash management account in her name that returns a few hundred dollars interest each year.

Alexander converted his $400,000 superannuation money (15 per cent is a tax free component) into an account based pension on 1 July in a self managed superannuation fund where he is the only member and he and Emma are both trustees. He plans to withdraw $20,000 (5 per cent) of his account balance as a tax free income stream this financial year. Alexander owns a residential rental property debt free in his own name valued at $600,000 that returns $29,500 net rent annually (after deducting expenses). He recently inherited $300,000 from an elderly aunt and as he can no longer contribute to superannuation he has placed this amount in a cash management account in his own name. He plans to transfer the whole amount to a term deposit that will earn $19,500 per annum. However, this is not a tax effective strategy, because if he does as he plans he will pay about $9,000 per annum in tax and Medicare levy.

A friend of the couple suggested they come to us for advice before Alexander proceeded with his plan. We recommended that as Emma was age 60 Alexander should contribute the $300,000 inheritance into an account for Emma in the self managed superannuation fund as a spouse contribution. He was a bit dubious about this at first because it was his inheritance. When we pointed out the benefit of working together as a couple to legally minimise their tax, and that the effect of this contribution would mean that his personal tax and Medicare levy liability would be reduced to nil after the senior Australians tax offset had been applied, he was very happy with the idea. We advised him that he should make sure that Emma does not exceed her non-concessional contribution cap over a three year period so that she can use the bring-forward rule for the $300,000 without penalty.

The spouse contribution is treated as a non-concessional contribution in the fund. As Alexander will have a tax liability this year when he adds the interest he earned on the cash management account to his rental income he can claim an 18 per cent tax offset for the first $3,000 of spouse contributions. That is a $540 tax offset which will reduce his tax liability. We also suggested that Emma should start an account based pension immediately and she plans to withdraw $12,000 this year.

Their tax position will be:

	Alexander	Emma	Combined
Income stream	$20,000	$12,000	$32,000
	tax free	tax free	tax free
Rental income	$29,500	Nil	$29,500
Interest income	$2,000	$500	$2,500
Taxable income	$31,500	$500	$32,000
Less tax (excludes Medicare levy and tax offsets)	$3,825	Nil	$500
After-tax income	$47,675	$12,500	$60,175

With the spouse contribution strategy, Alexander and Emma have increased their combined after-tax income to $60,175.

APPROACHING YOUR RETIREMENT DATE

As you approach retirement you need to make a decision about your superannuation savings. Decisions may involve taking your superannuation as a lump sum at retirement and then investing it in your own name. Another option would be to roll your superannuation benefits into a 'transition to retirement income stream' whilst the benefits are preserved. Once you reach your preservation age and retire or reach age 65 the benefits will become unpreserved and become an account based income stream.

Even if your retirement is some years off, you may be able to access some of your superannuation while you're still working. Here's how.

TRANSITION TO RETIREMENT INCOME STREAMS

If you have reached your preservation age, which is age 55 if you were born before 1 July 1960, you can withdraw some of your superannuation whilst you are still working as a transition to retirement income stream. This is particularly useful if you want to reduce your working hours but not your income. In addition it allows you to take advantage of the tax concessions available to superannuation income streams. Even if you are not reducing your working hours you may still choose to access some of your superannuation as a transition to retirement income stream once you turn age 60 because the income is tax free and you may want to use it to reduce non-deductible debt. In fact this is a good option to get rid of outstanding credit card debts and other non-deductible debts quickly.

If your accumulating superannuation is with a large superannuation fund that provides superannuation income streams (which most refer to as 'pensions') contact the fund to find out what you need to do to establish one. Decide how much superannuation you want to transfer to the transition to retirement income stream and the fund will establish it for you. If your superannuation is in a self managed superannuation fund you will need to get the necessary paperwork drawn up. As your financial situation is unique it is advisable to discuss whether this option is the best way for you to supplement your other income with your financial adviser and tax accountant.

While you continue to work your employer's and your own superannuation contributions can continue to be paid into your accumulating superannuation account.

The transition to retirement rules are:

— You must have reached your preservation age and also be under 65

— You can only take your preserved superannuation as a non-commutable (non-cashable) account-based pension and not as a lump sum

— If unpreserved benefits are used to establish the income stream these will be reduced first by the amount of income withdrawn each year

— The minimum withdrawal you can make each financial year
is 4 per cent of your account balance on 1 July (or a pro-
rata amount in the year of commencement if the start date
is not 1 July), unless reduced further by the government. (It
was reduced to 2 per cent in 2008-09 and 2009-10 to assist
people who had been adversely affected by the global
financial crisis to preserve more of their capital.)

— The maximum withdrawal you can make each financial year
until your benefits become unpreserved is 10 per cent of
your account balance on 1 July (or a pro-rata amount in the
year of commencement if the start date is not 1 July)

— You can only withdraw more than 10 per cent or convert
the remaining preserved amount to a lump sum:

  – if you meet a condition of release, such as permanent
    retirement or reaching age 65

  – to change the balance back to accumulation

  – to purchase another transition to retirement income
    stream.

If your superannuation is based on a defined benefit the amount
transferred to a transition to retirement income stream will be
transferred into an accumulation account and you will therefore need
to choose an investment option. You will bear the investment risks
and gain the investment benefits on the account balance underlying
the transition to retirement income stream. If you are a member of
a large fund and you have not chosen an investment option, your
accumulation account balance will be automatically invested in the
fund's default investment option, which is generally the balanced
option.

CREATE TAX FREE INCOME FOR RETIREMENT

When you roll over your superannuation money on retirement to a superannuation income stream, you defer or eliminate lump sum tax and any earnings in the fund are tax free. You can also receive an income stream that is taxed concessionally or that is tax free.

An account based superannuation income stream has two components which are the tax free amount and the taxable amount. The tax free amount is made up of after-tax personal contributions that have not been claimed as a tax deduction, spouse contributions and government co-contributions (it may also have a frozen amount calculated on 30 June 2007 relating to other components). The proportion of the tax free component in the income stream is calculated at the commencement of the income stream and remains constant. It has relevance whilst you are under age 60 and when you die. Each time you make withdrawals before your sixtieth birthday the assessable income is calculated using the taxable component proportion. A 15 per cent tax offset reduces the tax on the income stream for people who are age 55 to under age 60. This is illustrated in the example below.

Example: Reducing tax on an income stream. Margaret is retiring early at age 57 and doesn't intend to enter the workforce again. She has $600,000 in accumulated superannuation benefits in a taxed superannuation fund which has a tax free component of $150,000 (25 per cent of the account balance) and a taxable component of $450,000 (75 per cent of the account balance). She rolls over her superannuation money and commences an account based income stream on 1 July. She must withdraw a minimum amount of 4 per cent of the account balance on 1 July, that is $24,000. If she withdraws $24,000, $6,000 will be the tax free component and $18,000 will be the taxable component, and she can claim a tax offset amount of $2,700 ($18,000 x 15 per cent) against her overall tax liability. However, any excess unused tax offset is not refundable and so lost.

If she withdraws $48,000 income her income and tax offset amount will be:

Tax free component ($48,000 x 25 per cent)	$12,000
Taxable component (48,000 x 75 per cent)	$36,000
Taxable income	$36,000
15 per cent tax offset amount	$5,400

Any earnings in the account based pension account are exempt from tax. Any withdrawals Margaret makes after she reaches age 60 will be tax free and there will be no tax offset amount.

TAX PAYABLE WHEN YOU WITHDRAW SUPERANNUATION

Your superannuation fund will deduct any applicable tax before paying you your superannuation benefit. However you should still understand the rules before requesting a benefit is paid so you don't pay more tax than you need to. These are the tax withholding rules that apply to lump sum withdrawals of the taxed component from a taxed superannuation fund:

Lump sum withdrawals:

— **Under preservation age** (currently under age 55): 20 per cent of the taxable component (can only be withdrawn in specified approved circumstances)

— **Age 55 to 59:**
  - Low rate cap ($150,000 at the time of writing): no tax payable
  - Amount over the low rate cap: 15 per cent of the taxable component

— **Age 60 or more:** tax free.

Withdrawals as a superannuation income stream:

— **Age 55 to 59:** marginal tax rate less 15 per cent tax offset

— **Age 60 or more:** tax free

The tax free component is tax free regardless of your age. Medicare levy is also payable on the taxed component.

Withdraw and re-contribute to minimise tax

Non-concessional contributions can be very tax effective if they are made prior to retirement and prior to commencing a superannuation income stream. They increase the tax free proportion of the income stream whilst the person is under age 60 and can also reduce the tax payable on death if your superannuation is paid to a non-tax dependant such as your adult children.

If you are over age 55 and satisfy a condition of release and your superannuation money is in a taxed superannuation fund, you can withdraw a lump sum up to your superannuation benefits cap amount without paying tax. You can then re-contribute that amount as a non-concessional contribution to your fund before converting it to an account based income stream. This will reduce the proportion that is a taxable component you withdraw each year until you reach age 60, at which time the income will be tax free.

Be warned, though, you should always get professional advice before carrying out a withdrawal and re-contribution strategy to ensure you do it correctly without breaching any of the rules.

Example: Withdrawal and re-contribution of the low rate superannuation benefits cap. Shirley is 56 years old. She is divorced with two adult children and has just retired early. She has $250,000 of superannuation money all from employer and salary sacrifice contributions plus earnings. She wants to commence an account based pension and also minimise her overall tax liability. She receives $15,600 net rental income from her investment unit in the city.

In order to minimise tax on her superannuation income stream she is advised to withdraw $150,000 of her superannuation benefit and reinvest it back into her superannuation account. She then rolls over her superannuation money into an account based income stream. She wants to withdraw $25,000 in the first year.

Her tax position will be:

	Without withdrawal and re-contribution	With withdrawal and re-contribution
Taxable component of income stream	$25,000	$10,000
Net rental income	$15,600	$15,600
Taxable income	**$40,600**	**$25,600**
Estimated tax	$5,100	$1,600
Less income stream tax offset	$3,750	$1,500
Tax payable	**$1,350**	**$100**
Tax free income	Nil	$15,000

Her overall tax saving is approximately $1,250.

By implementing this simple strategy, Shirley will reduce her overall tax by about $1,250 and will pay less Medicare levy. In addition when she dies her children will only pay tax on 40 per cent of the remaining superannuation instead of paying tax on the whole amount.

Other potential uses of a re-contribution strategy

A re-contribution strategy prior to age 60 may provide a better tax outcome for a superannuation death benefit if the deceased is under aged 60 at the date of death or if the beneficiary has not reached age 60.

A re-contribution strategy reduces the taxable component of a future superannuation death benefit that may be paid to a non-tax dependant. Since non-tax dependants, such as adult children, pay tax on the taxable component of a superannuation death benefit, a re-contribution strategy will save tax by increasing a member's tax free component where there is a possibility that upon death a non-tax dependant would be a beneficiary.

In order to make the most out of these superannuation strategies, get advice from a competent superannuation specialist or adviser before you proceed. You never know, there could be better alternatives for your particular circumstances.

Our last words

We do congratulate you on taking the journey through this book. Perhaps you have read the book straight through or only specific sections that apply to your own stage of life. Either way we wish to end this book with a few final words.

As we have said in our previous books, we have never met anyone who plans to stop living when they retire, yet we meet many who fail to plan for that time.

In short, do what needs to be done by taking these specific actions to achieve your early retirement plan:

— Make a budget and stick to it

— Pay off your debts

— Save more and spend less

— Invest, diversify and protect your money

— Educate yourself in financial and investment matters and get advice where necessary.

Money can't buy you happiness or health but it certainly improves your lifestyle.

It's your life, it's your retirement lifestyle, make the most of your money and your life whilst you are here!

Use and apply the information from this and our other books to your own circumstances. It will help you to:

— Retire earlier than you otherwise could

— Save tax

— Increase your retirement income

— Have the dignity and lifestyle that you want and deserve for the rest of your life.

Your future is in your hands. If you want to retire early, start planning to build your retirement savings now by maintaining a long term view. You need to respond carefully to:

— Economic changes, (e.g. interest rates, inflation rates, etc.)

— Changes in investment markets, (e.g. market booms and downturns and busts) and changes in legislation

— Changes in your own personal circumstances, (e.g. marriage, unemployment, children, divorce, death in the family, and so on).

Be happy now and in retirement. Life is for living, it's not a dress rehearsal. Enjoy each moment for what it is, whatever it is and maximise your retirement savings and income. Then when you are retired, SKI – Spend Your Kids Inheritance (if you don't they will)!

Barbara Smith and Ed Koken
www.oasiswealth.com.au

Appendix

This Appendix contains the tax rates, thresholds and deeming rates that have been referred to in this book that applied when this book went to press in March 2010. Some may be subject to indexing or change in the future.

VARIOUS CHAPTERS

Marginal tax rates for resident individuals:

$0 to $6000	Nil
$6001 to $35,000	15%
$35,001 to $80,000	30%
$80,001 to $180,000	38%
$180,001 and over	45%

CHAPTER 7

Concessional contributions cap in the financial year:

Member's age	Concessional contributions cap
Under 50	$25,000 indexed*
50 to under 75 until 30 June 2012	$50,000 unindexed

Non-concessional contributions cap in the financial year:

Member's age	Concessional contributions cap
Under 65	$150,000** (option to bring forward contribution of up to $450,000 in a three year period)
65 to under 75	$150,000, no option to bring forward

Superannuation benefits cap

$150,000 indexed*

*Indexed by average weekly ordinary time earnings and increased by $5,000 only when the aggregate amount is at least $5,000
** fixed at six times the concessional contributions cap

CHAPTER 8

The rate of pension is calculated under both the income and assets tests with the test that results in the lower pension rate applying.

The income and assets tests are applied to the combined value of the basic pension rates and pension supplement. The following rates and thresholds are current at the time of writing this book in March 2010. Please check the Centrelink website for the current rates and thresholds.

Maximum age and service age pension rates per fortnight from 20 March 2010

	Single and illness separated couple (each)	Couple both eligible (combined)	Couple one partner eligible
Maximum basic rate	$644.20	$971.20	$485.60
Maximum pension supplement	$56.90	$85.80	$42.90
Total	$701.10	$1057,00	$528.50

Income and Assets tests

Income test for pensions per fortnight

Family situation	Allowable income for full pension**
Single	up to $142.00
Single + one child	up to $166.60
Couple (combined)	up to $248.00
Illness separated couple (combined)	up to $248.00
Additional children	add $24.60 per child

**Income over these amounts reduces by 50¢ in the dollar for single pensioners and 25¢ in the dollar each for couples

Assets test for homeowners and transitional homeowners from 1 January 2010

Family situation	Allowable assets for full pension*
Single	up to $178,000
Couple (combined)	up to $252,500
Illness separated couple (combined)	up to $252,500
One partner eligible	up to $252,500

Assets test for non-homeowners and transitional non-homeowners

Family situation	Allowable assets for full pension*
Single	up to $307,000
Partnered (combined)	up to $381,500
Illness separated couple (combined)	up to $381,500
One partner eligible	up to $381,500

*Assets over these amounts reduce age pension payments by $1.50 per fortnight for every $1,000 above the limit (single and couple combined).

Deeming rates from 20 March 2010

Single and getting either a pension or allowance:

- the first $42,000 of financial investments is deemed to earn income at 3 per cent per annum
- amount over $42,000 is deemed to earn income at 4.5 per cent per annum.

Member of a couple and:

1. one or both members are getting a pension:
   - the first $70,000 (combined) of financial investments is deemed to earn income at 3 per cent per annum
   - amount over $70,000 is deemed to earn income at 4.5 per cent per annum

2. neither is getting a pension:
   - the first $35,000 for each of you and your partner's financial investments is deemed to earn income at 3 per cent per annum
   - amount over $35,000 is deemed to earn income at 4.5 per cent per annum.

CHAPTER 9

Co-contribution thresholds for the 2010 financial year:

Minimum income threshold amount	$31,920
Maximum income threshold amount	$61,920

Index

Accessing Smith and Koken's expertise

Barbara Smith and Ed Koken's expertise is available to help people set up and manage their own tax structures – including a full self managed superannuation fund establishment package, self managed income streams and trusts – and to work out tax-effective retirement strategies that maximise retirement income.

If you are interested in self managed super or one of the income streams or strategies discussed in this book you can contact Barbara and Ed for a fee-based consultation.

Barbara Smith and Ed Koken are based in Melbourne and run a financial services business called Oasis Wealth (AFSL No. 293770). Both are qualified accountants, registered tax agents and financial advisers. They are the authors of many books on self managed superannuation, retirement planning, tax and superannuation.

Barbara Smith and Ed Koken are ready to help you with all of the following services:

- Fee-based advice on tax-saving strategies
- Preparation of accounts and tax returns for self managed superannuation funds
- Preparation of individual, trust and company tax returns
- Investment and business structure advice
- Superannuation planning
- Establishing a self managed superannuation fund with individuals or a company as trustee including applications and paperwork
- Retirement planning and tax strategies for retirement
- Self managed super fund income stream establishment, advice and compliance work
- Full and frank advice tailored to your tax, superannuation and retirement planning needs.

For more details on any of these services or books, call Barbara or Ed on (03) 9457 1016, write to PO Box 2039, Ivanhoe East Vic 3079, or email smith.koken@optusnet.com.au or visit <www.oasiswealth.com.au>.

Readers of this book are enititled to a free one-year subscription to the authors' quarterly eNewsSheet. Just send an email with the subject line "Free subscription for 1 year" to superbsmith@optusnet.com.au. Please note that emails sent to this address are not opened.

major st
PUBLISHING

If you have enjoyed reading this book you might like to visit our website www.majorstreet.com.au or become a fan on our Major Street Publishing Facebook page.